MUSICIAN!

A Practical Guide for Students, Music Lovers, Amateurs, Professionals, Superstars, Wannabees and Has-Beens

Dan Wilensky

Speechless Productions
New York, NY
July, 2010

Cover design by Tony Halpin
Back cover photo by Peter Orkin
Back page illustration by Joy Price

LCCN: 2010910544
ISBN: 1452857717
ISBN-13: 9781452857718

Printed in the United States of America

For my family.

CONTENTS

PART 1: NUTS AND BOLTS   1

Music is Good For Kids
How and why to encourage a young musician.

It's a Wonderful Life
A happy tale to inspire you.

The Care and Feeding of Your Instrument
10 quick tips.

An Hour a Day
My One Hour Practice Routine For Beginners, Hobbyists and Jaded Professionals.

A Mind is a Terrible Thing to Waste
Learn to learn.

There's Music in the Air
Use your ear. Listening is an art.

The Wise Man Knows You Should Compose
Learn to write music.

Mommy, Where Do Gigs Come From?
How and where to find work.

Beyond the Notes
Learn from singers. "Lose" yourself.

I Can't Go On . . .
Learn to manage your stage fright.

Are We Having Fun Yet?
Add humor to your music.

Space is the Place
Avoid "note-itis" and learn to back up singers.

Style-Hopping
Sound good in multiple contexts.

So You Want To Be a Studio Musician
The trials and tribulations of studio work.

Be You Ever So Humble
Remain modest under duress.

One Good Discipline Deserves Another
Enhance your musical abilities with non-musical activities.

So Much To Learn
Take lessons and teach.

Sing, Sing, Sing
Singing is good for you.

A Critique of Critics
Ignore most music critics.

PART 4: PHILOSOPHICAL AND SPIRITUAL GUIDANCE 97

Remember Me?
What to do when your career slows down or falls apart.

Abandon Ship!
Why and when to throw in the towel.

Why Are You (or Why Do You Want to Be) a Musician?
Well....?

Baptism of Fire
Beyond music and money.

The Big Easy
The big debacle.

There is *No* Grass on the Other Side of the Fence
Jumping ship too soon.

Nice Day For A White Wedding
Right time, wrong place.

Game Over
Delusions of athletic grandeur.

Spilled Champagne
Missed opportunities and other boo-boos.

Bright Moments
Glory stories.

ACKNOWLEDGMENTS

My heartfelt thanks go to Emily Benedek, Vicki Genfan, Jean Howson, Paul Jacobs, Rick Kriska, Rich Mercurio, Jeff Mironov, Tim Ouimette, Saundra Schlink, Darren Solomon, Jeff Wyman, and the anonymous director in Riverside Park. Their wisdom, generosity and encouragement were invaluable.

I am forever indebted to my teachers, students, employers, colleagues and fans who have enriched my life and given me something to write about.

Finally, my deepest gratitude goes to my parents and my brothers who, in addition to providing love, records and music lessons, also tolerated much cacophony.

Without music, life is a journey through a desert.

– Pat Conroy

The music business is a cruel and shallow money trench, a long plastic hallway where thieves and pimps run free, and good men die like dogs. There's also a negative side.

– Hunter S. Thompson

PREFACE

Learn ...

* How to encourage a young musician.
* How to become and remain inspired.
* How to listen and how to use what you hear.
* How to make music more than a hobby and still have fun.
* How to make money playing and writing music.
* How to get along with your employers and colleagues.
* How to build an effective stage presence.
* How to catapult your playing to a new level.
* How to land the choice gigs.
* How to handle both success and failure.

And much more.

This is a book for all musicians, and anyone who loves music. My goal is to boost anyone who plays an instrument to a higher plateau – eventually to heights that they merely dreamed of. For the neophyte, I try to demystify the process of becoming a "real" musician. For the typical late-night club musician I provide a list of reasons and ways to advance. For the fortunate elite among you, I share my insights on how to capture and maintain the elusive creative fire that separates the journeyman from the virtuoso. For the general reader, I include humorous stories and anecdotes from the Wild Wild West that is the music business. From nurturing young musicians to helping professionals cultivate their own identity, I aim to examine familiar territory with a fresh perspective, and attempt to illuminate subjects that are rarely discussed.

Musician! addresses not only how to survive, but how to *flourish* in the music world. It provides specific examples of how to find work, how to listen and practice, how to get along with other musicians, how to promote yourself, how to survive and utilize competition and criticism, and how to deal with stage fright. It suggests what record companies can and cannot do for you, what you can learn, buy and sell using the Internet, which books to read and what equipment to buy, when to lay low or pursue non-musical activities, and why musicality is next to godliness. In *Tales From the Trenches* I recount war-stories about my early career faux pas that will assist you in avoiding similar mistakes. *Musician!* even includes helpful hints on how to manage your money, stay healthy, and succeed in romance while you pursue your musical dreams.

As the title of this book suggests, I've cast an extremely wide net: my aim is to include *something* for every musician, at every stage of their development, regardless of what kind of music they play. Inevitably there will be sections that won't apply to you. But I'd suggest that if you're a beginner, it wouldn't hurt to apply the more advanced ideas; if you're a seasoned pro, you'll benefit by reviewing the simpler lessons. I hope that this book will be fun to read; musicians tend to take themselves way too seriously. But there's also a need for a musician's guide that is not dumbed down.

Obviously your life and career experiences are going to be different from mine. But after 30 years in the music business, I've made enough mistakes, won enough battles, and played enough gigs to pass on some practical advice. Of course, the warning "do as I say, not as I do" has never been more applicable; I've set a high standard and I'll need to follow my own advice.

It's impossible to fully describe the euphoria that can occur when you're "at one" with your instrument, or when you play with great musicians in front of an enthusiastic audience. And no one knows the blues like a brilliant but unemployed musician; attempting to *talk* about the blues is a losing battle. In fact, as I discuss later, talking or writing about any kind of music is a clumsy endeavor which pales next to *making* music. Even in its recorded form, music doesn't stand still long enough to be accurately portrayed by mere words. But if someone has to write a book on "musicianhood," it probably helps if he's a bona fide music veteran.

One reason I wrote this book is that when I was a teenager, I wanted to find a consolidated source of "real life" information for the average musician that wasn't simply a superstar's tell-all, a lawyer or manager's music biz manifesto, a playing or practicing method, or yet another homage to technology. When you're starting out, you need guidance from a pro who remembers what it's like to be green. Similarly, if you've been successful but have reached a dead end, it helps when a peer who's experienced similar lows suggests proactive and imaginative ways to move forward. In addition to having experienced many career and artistic peaks and valleys, I have an enduring love for all types of music and musicians; I can't imagine pursuing any other life. So for me, writing this book was a way of sharing my unbridled passion for music and giving you a practical, and I hope entertaining, all-in-one guide.

There is, of course, no substitute for getting out there and playing with other musicians in front of an audience – an art that is sometimes under-appreciated, and, indeed, occasionally in danger of extinction. You'll learn more in one night on the bandstand than any book can teach you; finding your *own* methods for negotiating the music maze is half the battle. But *Musician!* shows you what to look for, and suggests ways to exploit your discoveries on and off the bandstand.

This book contains numerous business and marketing strategies, but before you concentrate on selling yourself, you should make great music. Although both disciplines are essential to your success, an obsession with selling can consume your creative energy. And we're all sick of advertisements. The phone will probably ring more often when you play music that you love, and word gets around that you sounded inspired on your last gig.

If you too are a music biz veteran, you know how easy it is to lose your soul in the abyss of the entertainment industry and to forget why you became a musician in the first place. For those of you who have "lost your way" I've included ideas that should help you refresh your creative spirit. If you're an amateur or part-time musician, I hope that reading this book will either enhance your enjoyment of music or will help you become a full-time professional. Obviously you will have to do most of the work: although this book gives you tips on recognizing and capitalizing on the important opportunities that come your way, you must create those opportunities by practicing and gigging relentlessly.

Implementing some of my suggestions requires money; others simply demand hard work, confidence or discipline. But don't forget serendipity: luck now plays a bigger role than ever in your quest to leave your day job or to maintain creative autonomy. Guitar sales are up, membership in high school marching bands is on the rise and enrollment in music schools is increasing – all at a time when the demand for skilled musicians is dwindling. Where will you find a gig? Don't worry about it. By the time you read this, things will have changed yet *again*, so my suggestion is: practice hard, believe in yourself, and let the soft shoe of destiny kick you where it may.

Though I've included a one hour practice routine, I do not suggest specific scales, exercises or songs for you to practice, as I assume you'll practice everything. And though *The Next Plateau* chapter contains a few listening suggestions, I've chosen not to include an "essential discography" list: I assume you will *listen* to everything. You should surround yourself with music, music books, and musical instruments; go to concerts; listen and play something new every day; eat and breathe music. Then take a vacation.

In summary, I hope *Musician!* will prove to be a valuable addition to your library – a reader-friendly reference book that you can use and enjoy throughout the many phases of your career.

Now go practice!

PART 1:
NUTS AND BOLTS

*A broad range of suggestions for beginners,
professionals, and everyone in-between.*

Music is Good For Kids

The debate continues on whether musical "talent" is congenital. I believe that one day, scientists will isolate a music-specific gene (or at least a talent protein) that will explain musical genius. I'm much more interested in the creative potential of children; it's never too early or too late to nurture their inherent creativity.

The ancient Greeks believed that a child's education should begin with music because it encompasses so many disciplines, and stimulates even the youngest minds. Though the ancients also had a narrow definition of what constitutes "good" music, I think they were on the right track. There is now definitive evidence that music played or sung during late pregnancy and in the first few months of life speeds up language development and gives children so exposed an advantage in physical and cognitive development that lasts.

Music cultivates advanced listening and math skills; it promotes hand-eye coordination and physical confidence; it provides an outlet for self expression and emotional release; it utilizes both sides of the brain. Reading music requires learning a new language; playing music with other people demands sensitivity, patience, and cooperation; kids often increase their appreciation for all of the arts when they learn to make music.

Encourage young musicians in every way you can. Help them to experience music viscerally – to feel and love music. If you have a child (or any young relative or friend), make sure that they have access to at least one instrument. For toddlers, you can construct cost-effective drum sets from household items, like old washboards or boxes; anything that makes an interesting sound when jostled or smacked will do. Many companies make cheap and durable recycled plastic instruments that are surprisingly pleasing to the ear. Recorders, harmonicas, Kazoos, and melodicas are also good instruments for young kids. Sing with them. Play musical games with them. Help them to explore rhythm and movement. *Surround* them with music.

Every child is ready to try a "real" instrument as soon as they can hold one. Hopefully, your local school system has a thriving music program that provides free instruments for its students, but if not, check with your local music store for rent-to-buy instruments; rentals are often inexpensive and give kids a chance to decide which instrument they like best. If they suddenly lose interest, try again in six months. For birthdays, graduations, and holidays consider giving a child a musical instrument instead of the latest computer game.

Then buy your future musician an iPod, tape recorder, vinyl records, and sheet music; take him to free outdoor music festivals, and concerts and clubs that allow minors; help him participate in school music programs; keep your radio tuned to high quality stations and give him a radio of his own so he can listen to whatever he pleases. (I'll never forget the magic of listening to my first transistor radio – I felt so hip!) Find him a good private teacher or two. Give him play-along records [Jamey Aebersold Jazz, Inc., 800-456-1388, is an excellent source for these]. Provide biographies of great musicians. Even if you don't produce a musical wunderkind, you'll have enriched a child's life immeasurably.

A little support goes a long way: tell young people that they sound wonderful, especially when they are beginners or when they sound less than mellifluous. Foster and feed even the slightest musical inclinations; for some kids, it's a remarkable achievement when they simply learn how to assemble and care for their instrument properly. Others need to learn how to play with other musicians, and should be given every chance to do so. I've known many children who didn't get along with their siblings and schoolmates *until* they started playing music. Also, if your protégé tires of one instrument, and wants to learn another one, give him your blessing.

Continue to make your child's musical education a joyful experience by allowing him to learn and listen to any type of music he desires in addition to practicing scales and études. When I became frustrated during my early piano lessons, my first teacher assigned simple arrangements of Vince Guaraldi's music for the *Charlie Brown* TV shows, and other familiar tunes. This never failed to motivate me to practice. If your kid wants to play music by The Rolling Stones instead of Chopin, so be it. Just make sure she has a place to practice that is far away from your office and your bedroom, or buy some earplugs.

Music makes both the performer and the audience feel good. When a child realizes that when she plays she delights her friends, parents and other adults, it inspires her to play more. This healthy ego massage is particularly helpful to kids who lack confidence, or who have other emotional problems. And as perhaps the most abstract art, music has no match for sparking and expanding the imagination.

One of the most helpful things you can do for all the children in your area is to contribute to school music programs or at least attend school concerts. Believe in the "4 Rs": Reading, 'Riting, 'Rithmatic and *Rhythm*. Let the teachers and the school board know how important music is to you, and show your appreciation to the music teachers who are doing their job well. Contribute to VH1 Save The Music (212-846-7600). These actions are needed more than ever because funding for school music programs is on the endangered species list (see *So Much To Learn*).

The effort that you put into the musical education of a child pays unlimited dividends.

It's a Wonderful Life

Before we examine the many evil demons and scary monsters in the netherworld of the music biz, let's take a look at the end of the rainbow – of dreams coming true. Here's a sweet tale from my early halcyon days.

I close my eyes and I see the ancient homes, olive trees, terraces and fishing ports of Sardinia – a magical island in the Mediterranean. We have arrived on a gorgeous July day to play at an outdoor amphitheater; colorful posters of our band are everywhere, and people stop us to practice their English and to tell us how much they love our record. The concert promoter whisks us away to a restaurant carved out of a hillside where a few local musicians, artists and officials are awaiting our arrival; an enormous oak table has been set with wine, bread, fresh olive oil from the trees in the distance, cheese to end all cheese, bowls of colorful fruit – and this is the first course. The conversation is fascinating, but the dessert is even better.

After this extraordinary four-hour cultural and culinary extravaganza, the band trundles up a hill via ancient cobblestone streets to the original Borcelino hat store. We try on what seems like every item in the store, buy three hats and several "gangster" suits, and saunter down the hill to our hotel to sleep it off.

Around 6:30, our phones ring in the haze of a crazy dream or two. Cold water on the face and the smell of coffee in the lobby help move things along. The promoter and his assistant pass out triple espressos to-go and we head off to the sound check. Along the way the promoter gives us a mini-tour, and tells us the history of Sardinia, complete with fascinating profiles of many of the older residents we pass along the way. After an unusually efficient sound check (for rural Italy), we have a "little snack" at a nearby café. A warm breeze envelops us.

Concerts in Italy go one of two ways: fantastico, or disastroso. Our band is 'on' tonight and we experience the former. After five encores, with the summer sea magic still in the air, we leave the stage and are immediately surrounded by effusive fans, most of who invite us to their homes for a midnight dinner. When our manager manages to break through the crowd, she informs us that we've been invited to the premier seafood restaurant on the island, which has been reserved for the exclusive use of the band and its guests. We pile into the van in two seconds, with friends in tow. At the top of another, taller hill with dramatic views of the coastline, we walk into the four-star restaurant and see a glorious table holding a giant fresh swordfish surrounded by every Italian delicacy imaginable. More superb wine is poured, and plates are passed; a local band has been hired for our pleasure; we eat, drink, dance, and sing the night away.

The next day, our pictures are on the front page of the local newspaper with the headline, "Viva New York Music." Life in the music business – when it's good – is *really* good.

This was just one of the many remarkable 24 hours that the music world has bestowed upon me. No superlatives can accurately describe the feeling you experience when the music, the audience, the business, the location, the weather, and the extracurricular activities mesh in your favor. Sometimes it's so darn good that you feel guilty. Nirvana-on-earth does exist! For me, skipping most of my after-school "hangs" to practice the saxophone was more than worth it. Give it a college try – you might get lucky.

But the unfortunate truth is that most gigs are not as easy, enjoyable or glamorous as my Sardinia experience. You might often have to play music that you don't particularly enjoy. Many jobs require a lot of schlepping and waiting around. At least half of all sound systems and room acoustics are terrible. Traveling, eating on the run, and playing for small or unappreciative audiences all take their toll. And at the end of it all, the pay might not be commensurate with the time, energy, expertise, and plain old hard work that you've contributed. I've had plenty of gigs – even months – where *nothing* went right. Reaching the very top is less likely than joining the NBA. The point is to learn how to handle both your successes and failures with grace. Later on in *Tales From The Trenches* you can read about some of my rough gigs and bad decisions, and what I learned from them.

Now for the meat and potatoes ...

The Care and Feeding of Your Instrument

1) Buy the best equipment you can possibly afford, and keep your instruments in tip-top shape. Some instruments – violins, for instance – sound better the more you play them.

2) Find a repair person who does quality work for everyone, not just his famous clients. This might take a little research and experimentation.

3) Learn basic repair and maintenance techniques that you can perform on the fly.

4) Read the music trade papers and pay attention to the equipment reviews and ads.

5) Visit a music store regularly to try gear, pick up supplies, and chat with the staff about what devices other musicians are using.

6) Keep an eye out for inexpensive used equipment on eBay and Craigslist. MusiciansFriend.com is a good place to buy new gear.

7) In addition to basic essentials, like a sturdy road case, buy more recent devices – wireless systems and slick new effects – that will give you an edge in the marketplace (see *Man and Machine*).

8) After you get a few big gigs under your belt, try to get endorsement deals with your favorite companies.

9) Handle your instrument with loving care. Keep it clean. Treat it as though it were your own baby. While you're at it, handle *yourself* with care; you are the most important instrument.

10) One of my students fell asleep at a movie theater with his vintage Selmer saxophone by his side. When he awoke, it had vanished. It had taken him five months to save enough to buy it, and five minutes to lose it. The horn wasn't insured.

Buy instrument insurance. Make sure that your policy includes a "floater" clause, which insures your instruments when you take them out of your home. Also get your instruments re-appraised every few years so that they are insured for their full current value. As with all insurance policies, a lower deductible (the amount *not* covered – let's say the first $100) means a higher yearly premium, but in this case it's probably worth it; your instrument is more likely to be damaged than stolen, and it's helpful to have your insurance company cover that $350 repair bill. The American Federation of Musicians (AFM) offers low-cost instrument insurance, and there are several companies that specialize in policies for performing artists. Hold on to that ax!

An Hour a Day

Many of us lead busy lives that leave little time for practicing. But I believe that you can become fairly proficient at practically any discipline if you work at it for an hour every day for one or two years. You probably won't become a leader in your field this way, but you will eventually hold your own in a variety of contexts. Below is my **One Hour Practice Routine for Beginners, Hobbyists, and Jaded Professionals**. This regimen is applicable to most instruments but can be modified according to need. This routine will obviously be old hat for some of you, but do it anyway!

MINUTES / WHAT TO PRACTICE

10 / Play long tones. Work on your tonguing, picking, touch or bow technique.
 5 / Play the chromatic scale and various chromatic exercises.
10 / Practice Scales and arpeggios: major, minor, diminished, whole tone, and pentatonic.
 5 / Get up and stretch. Take some deep breaths.
10 / Sight read.
10 / Work on a new piece of music or memorize a new melody.
10 / Improvise, doodle, play with a CD or the radio.

Obviously, schedule permitting, you should increase the time you devote to each discipline. Some people find it helpful to do several short practice sessions, e.g. 20 minutes, three or four times a day. Whichever way you do it, the important thing is to do it *every day*, come rain or come shine. And remember: *don't give yourself a concert*. If your neighbors aren't complaining, you're probably not practicing.

A Mind is a Terrible Thing to Waste

Unfortunately, many musicians (not just guitar players and drummers) don't know how to read music, or don't read well. Unless you're dyslexic, this is inexcusable; all musicians should be proficient readers. Though neither Elvis Presley nor Jimi Hendrix could read music, don't convince yourself that you can get away with the same deficiency. When you become a good reader (and sight-reader), you will multiply your job possibilities and expand your musical horizon. If you intend to be a studio musician, know that there will be times when you're required to sight-read difficult music in a high-pressure environment – sometimes early in the morning (see *So You Want To Be a Studio Musician*).

Music is a language. Study hard until you learn the basic "grammar," "spelling," and "pronunciation" – then sight-read everything you can get your hands on, even material that is too difficult for you to play well. Do it for an hour every day and you'll see a noticeable improvement. If you're a beginner, music flash cards can be helpful. They're inexpensive, portable, easy to use, and they're the best way to improve your rote memory – half the reading battle (the other half being hand-eye coordination). There are also several computer programs available that teach you the basics, and test your knowledge.

It helps to see the big picture when you read music: think in terms of phrases and sections, not just individual notes. In addition, try to read ahead; as you play a note, your eye should be at least two notes ahead of that one. But there are no real secrets to becoming a sharp reader. Just do it all the time.

After you get a handle on reading music, begin (or continue) the lifelong study of melody, harmony and rhythm. I'm assuming that you're already practicing all your scales in all keys. If you're not, get started! Though I could easily devote an entire chapter to other aspects of music "anatomy," I will instead suggest that you hit your local library and music store, and scour the Web. There are numerous books and magazines at all levels that are devoted to this subject. And, as I discuss later, you're never too smart and it's never too late to go back to school, or to take private lessons. Some of my best students are retirees who want to keep growing, and realize that playing music keeps them young.

Memorize as many melodies as you can using your CDs and MP3s, the radio, "fake" books and play-along records. A good melody contains multiple lessons on harmony, rhythm, phrasing, and "note-efficiency" – saying more with less. Never stop building your repertoire. Play new songs with your fellow musicians as often as possible. Revisit the most difficult material until it becomes second nature.

Then, learn to improvise – especially if you're a classical musician with no prior training in that discipline. A great deal of the "magic" in music occurs when musicians improvise. Effective improvisation – composing on the fly – requires a few acts of faith: faith in your own creative and technical abilities; faith in your fellow musicians' support and sensitivity; fearless faith in the unknown. You must embrace the abstract. At its highest level, improvisation demands equal measures of knowledge, technique, inspiration, and instinct. But even the most rudimentary attempts at improvising can open the ears and expand the mind.

One exercise that I recommend for all musicians, regardless of their level of expertise, is to come up with as many motifs as possible using any four notes. Play the notes in any order, and feel free to repeat, bend, and accent them in various ways. Focus on rhythm, and use different tempos. When you tire of four-note combinations, add a fifth and so on. You'll be surprised at how much music you can make within these "walls." You'll be in good company too: Bach knew a thing or two about jamming on a riff.

Desmond Morris addressed this subject in his book *The Naked Ape* (1967):

EXPLORATION PLAY RULES

1) You shall investigate the unfamiliar until it has become familiar.
2) You shall impose rhythmic repetition on the familiar.
3) You shall vary this repetition in as many ways as possible.
4) You shall select the most satisfying of these variations and develop these at the expense of others.
5) You shall combine and recombine these variations one with another.
6) You shall do all this for its own sake, as an end in itself.

Next, study the blues, the ideal musical form to facilitate your improvisational skills: everyone has the blues; the 12 bar form is easy to understand and work with; the blues scale (C, Eb, F, Gb, G, Bb) sounds great unadorned; the blues is the basis for many musical forms, including rock, pop, and jazz; it's a great way to express yourself. Also, for many gigs you must be able to improvise over one chord and captivate the listener with your rhythmic and harmonic expertise. You can never practice blues and one-chord improvisation enough.

Then study the venerable art of jazz because it will open up your ears like no other music: Jazz is comprised of a panoply of harmonic and rhythmic techniques and concepts; it encompasses many musical styles while being completely unique; it thrives from and teaches disciplined individual expression, collective cooperation, and advanced sensitivity; jazz is seductive, cerebral, and satisfying to play; it's arguably the United States' most important contribution to world culture. I think of jazz as an advanced conversation – spontaneous, intelligent and passionate repartee based on fact, opinion, and imagination; a multidimensional melodic and rhythmic dialogue between sophisticated musicians; the summit where composition and improvisation meet. And it sounds good! After you master the basics, the world will be your oyster. Incidentally, I appreciate (and play) everything from Folk music to Funk, Reggae to Rumba, and Amadeus to Zeppelin, so please don't label me a jazz snob, or anything close.

If you don't like jazz or are intimidated by it, listen to it more. There's a vast jazz repertoire and a rich recorded legacy to explore. If nothing else, study jazz because it's challenging: Jazz musicians are basically embellishing a melody and elaborating on a theme using a defined musical structure – in real time; composing on the fly. Listen to any Louis Armstrong record to hear the penultimate examples of this skill. It is this instant invention – often at breakneck speed – that can be daunting to the neophyte. But *you* don't have to play it fast. Even before you begin formal studies, try playing a single chord on a piano with your left hand. Then with your right hand, play individual notes that sound good to you, and try to invent short melodies.

Jazz has come a long way since 1921 when Dr. Henry van Dyke said, "Jazz music was invented by demons for the torture of imbeciles." If you agree with Dr. van Dyke, perhaps learning more about jazz will change your mind. If not, go back to the blues.

All of these activities – sight-reading, learning music theory and harmony, memorizing melodies, and improvising – complement one another, and will help you become a complete musician. But nothing is more important than nurturing and nourishing your ear. Read on for more.

There's Music in the Air

Learn to listen. Listen to learn. Mean it when you say "I'm all ears."

Regardless of what style of music you play, learning entire songs – or their components – by ear is one of the best ways to improve your musicianship; you memorize the material more quickly and thoroughly, and uncover more musical layers than if you simply read it. When I was 17 I had the great privilege of studying with jazz legend Joe Henderson. During my first lesson, Joe taught me the first sixteen bars of John Coltrane's solo on "Countdown" by ear, one note at a time. Since the tempo was so fast and the harmonic structure so complex, I'd never dreamed of playing it, let alone memorizing it. I still know those sixteen bars better than any other piece of music.

If you keep your ears open you can pick up valuable musical information just by walking through a crowded city like New York or San Francisco: between the portable radios, street musicians, traffic sounds, and musicians practicing by open windows, the modern city provides a virtual encyclopedia of aural delights. Listen hard. There are bars with magnificent jukeboxes and restaurants with unusual CD collections; there's music in the diverse languages and voices of the people; college radio stations thrive. A recent notice for a Manhattan music festival reads like a trip around the world: "…there will be days and nights of tango and flamenco, songs from the streets of Naples, Korean masked dances, Gypsy music, Cuban music, Byzantine chant, Brazilian song, American folk, klezmer, Arab music, Judeo-Andalusian music from Morocco, Tibetan chants and a festival of Greek music and dance." Holy United Nations, Bat Man.

Take advantage of all the music in the air: play along with records, radios and televisions every day; imitate everything you hear. Do the best you can, and don't worry about playing wrong notes – they are your friends. Use them as reference points to find the correct notes: do you always miss by a certain interval? Stick with it – your ear will become more accurate and you'll learn to land on your feet. Turn on the radio, especially at night. When you go to sleep with music on, you're often able to recall and play snippets of what you heard in the haze of early slumber. (Don't use this technique as an excuse not to practice!) Turn up the TV and jam with movie soundtracks, jingles, theme songs and cartoons. This is one of the best ways to hear a smorgasbord of musical styles and to get an idea of what will be demanded of you when you do studio work (see *Style-Hopping* and *So You Want To Be a Studio Musician*).

Then, transcribe, transcribe, transcribe! Write down everything you hear – the chords, melodies, lyrics, grooves, solos – so that you can refer to it later. It doesn't matter whether you use an instrument to help or not. Try to notate the articulation, phrasing and dynamics correctly. Remain unfazed if you can't figure out certain sections of the piece – just leave blank bars. You can concentrate on a single element of the material if you like, e.g. the melody, but I recommend transcribing everything. iPods and other digital machines are ideal for this sort of work, as they can cycle a specific section of a song.

If it's the style of a particular instrumentalist you want to learn, there's no better way to do it than to meticulously transcribe her solos, and play them along with the recorded version, attempting to match her sound verbatim. When you transcribe a complex improvisation one note or phrase at a time, you're effectively internalizing an entire musical lexicon in slow motion. Then, when you then play it in real time – having absorbed so much harmonic and rhythmic information – you get the feeling that *you* are the improviser. Quite a sensation.

And it's not simply the transcription process that is useful. The content of the music you learn is equally important. Pick both music that you love, and music that you don't understand. When you're not performing you should copy, loot, cull, poach, and snatch every last bit of musical know-how you can – especially when you're young.

You should also make regular pilgrimages to hear superior music. This is easier said than done if you're playing all the time, and if you're unemployed you might hesitate to shell out $45 to hear a band when you could just listen to their grooves at home. But there's nothing like a good live show to fuel your desire to improve and fortify your belief that you can achieve greatness. Try to practice and write music soon after you hear a concert; the lessons you learn should be expressed in sound, not just by waxing positive to your friends. Also, the best musicians are constantly growing, and it's helpful to see them in various contexts and at various stages of their development. Going to clubs and concerts to catch your mentors in action is a wise use of your time and your money. Go get your live music fix.

However, don't *always* listen to learn; also listen to enjoy. Occasionally, turn off your intellect and be a fan. Turn on that "stupid" song or radio station that always makes you smile, and ignore the harsh comments from your colleagues and loved ones. There's nothing wrong with listening to music that makes you feel good.

Of course, silence *is* golden, and you shouldn't feel guilty for wanting to listen to the sound of silence on a regular basis too. Your ears (and your synapses) will thank you.

The Wise Man Knows You Should Compose

When I told a colleague of mine that I was writing a book on the ins and outs of musicianhood, he said, "The first advice I'd give to any musician is to learn how to compose." He's got a point. You'll stand a much better chance of making a good living in the music business if you add "composer" and "arranger" to your résumé.

There are numerous potential benefits to knowing how to write and arrange music: you will become a better musician; you will enhance your marketability; you can boost your current and future income by writing songs, jingles, TV themes, video game music and film scores; you can create a repertoire that best showcases your playing strengths; you can make a lasting contribution to the genre of music you love the most; you can express yourself beautifully without using words. If you also happen to be a skilled lyricist, you'll be unstoppable. Music composition is one of the highest art forms and has been an integral force in vibrant cultures throughout history. Join the party.

And a heck of party it is. Or was. If you had opened the door to one of the cubicles in the Brill building in New York in the late 50s and early 60s, you would have seen one of the great young songwriters of the day pounding out the hits. Imagine Jerry Lieber, Mike Stoller, Carole King, Jerry Goffin, Barry Mann, Cynthia Weil, Jeff Barry, Ellie Greenwich, Burt Bacharach, Hal David, Neil Sedaka and Doc Pommus all working under one roof! Then there was Motown. What do you say about Motown? There hasn't been anything like it since. In the past, publishers, record and film companies created *nurturing* environments for groups of composers and a ready market for their songs. Many of the department heads were accomplished musicians themselves – or at least had ears, and composers responded by writing what they knew and loved, *and* made money doing it. Songwriters are much more calculated and commerce-driven today – like most people. There are still plenty of great songs to be written – and obscene money to be made writing them – but the *vibe* of the party has changed.

Though there are still plenty of stories about songwriters whose first songs were hits, and quite a few untrained composers who have achieved commercial success, you should assume that you'll have to use more elbow grease than those lucky folks. Writing solid, original, and memorable music has never been easy, and getting your music heard often depends upon who you know; writing effective lyrics is *really* tough; and hit songs are the exception to the rule. But who said you need to write a hit song? As I mentioned, there are many reasons to write, and ways to generate income in the process (see *Mommy, Where Do Gigs Come From?*). First, learn the craft. Once you find your compositional voice, the rest will fall into place.

People often ask how I "come up with" my compositions. I explain that when I'm lucky, the music writes itself: I "hear" a song in a dream, wake up and furiously scribble it down or record it. Other ideas are born while I'm improvising, or jamming with other musicians. Sometimes I'll start a song, put it away, and combine it with other snippets years later. When I'm writing for hire, I let the project inspire me. But no matter how (or how well) you write, it's unlikely that you'll create something truly unique: most music is a patchwork of musical ideas accumulated over a lifetime. Just try to avoid overt plagiarism.

Whether or not you've ever tried to write music, you should jump in with both feet; get *something* down on paper or on tape. I've experienced both prolific spells and drout years, so I won't advise you to write every day, but write as much as you can. You should explore the many excellent books, periodicals, and websites devoted to songwriting and songwriters; take a composition and arranging class; find a mentor; find a writing partner who's at or above your level; analyze songs and scores; discover what makes your favorite music sound so good. You can get a great deal of inspiration directly from your MP3 collection, and from the radio. Also, visit ASCAP.com and BMI.com. There's a wealth of information on both sites.

Then, expect rejection – especially from your family and friends. The human ear is an extraordinarily subjective instrument: play a song for ten people and you may get eleven radically different opinions of it. Most people – including most music industry people – don't even *hear* the way you do, let alone have the same taste; it's their prerogative. Moreover, to the untrained or close-minded listener, one extraneous lick says "jazz," while one little backbeat shouts "rock." In other words, when you're ready to shop your wares, you need to pick your targets carefully. Eventually someone will hear things the way you do, or at least appreciate your sonic alchemy. Keep growing, and keep knocking on those doors.

Of course, many composers compose just to make money. If you're talented, well-connected and lucky, you might be able to score a publishing deal. The publisher (or record company) will get your songs to the right people. A 10% share of one moderately successful song can pay many bills. But I can't overemphasize how important it is to also write music that *you* like; when all is said and done, that's what matters most. If you make a few pennies in the process, so much the better. So what if you're not a Gershwin or a Porter. Be yourself! Just do us all a favor and throw in a good melody now and then. Or at least something we can dance to.

Once you learn to read and improvise, and learn the rudiments of composing and arranging, you'll be well-equipped to step out into the *real* music world where you'll find out what you *really* need to know. Read on for the details.

Mommy, Where Do Gigs Come From?

"Here comes everybody." – James Joyce

To find work as a musician you need skill, luck, good stage presence, networking skills, quick reactions, flexibility, tenacity, perseverance, and a somewhat likable personality. Then you need to street play … Street play?

I recorded my first jingle when I was nineteen, a direct result of playing my saxophone on the sidewalks of Madison Avenue. One woman who stopped to listen put five dollars into my open case and told me to call her regarding work. Assuming that she was just trying to be nice to a young street musician, I didn't expect much when I called her. Amazingly, she was a jingle contractor and she hired me for a Sugar Frosted Flakes spot the following week.

The previous year, right after graduating from Berkeley High, I toured with Ray Charles. This grand opportunity was courtesy of my friend Buddy Gordon, who I had met at a high school band competition. Buddy was playing lead trumpet with Ray, and he crashed at my place when the band came to town. The lead alto player had just quit, and Buddy said, "You should bring your horn to the club." Ten minutes before show time, I was asked to join the saxophone section backstage to play through a chart. Then the road manager handed me a suit that was three sizes too big and before I knew it, I was on stage with Brother Ray. I stayed for six months.

Fortunately, there are many other ways to find work. First, plant seeds: let *everyone* know that you're a musician, composer, bandleader – whatever – and make sure they have your number; always play like your life depended on it; sit in at clubs (see *Jammin' 'Til the Break of Dawn*); offer to perform at benefits, street fairs, schools and churches; play on song demos for free. Another idea is to hire several top-level musicians to rehearse and play one gig with you, and offer this "name band" to a club owner at no charge (few managers can resist this offer). Then, do a ton of promotion and play your tail off. This method, though potentially expensive, often pays significant dividends, even if you only find out how to do it better next time.

But by far the best and most direct way to find employment, is through other musicians, particularly those who play the same instrument as you. Cultivate relationships with players from the entire musical spectrum, and do sub work for them regardless of the wages or working conditions offered. If you're willing to do some long rehearsals and low-paying gigs, and maintain a positive attitude, better opportunities will arise: either your patron – pleased by your availability and reliability – will reward you with better jobs, or you'll meet a helpful person at the crummy jobs he gives you. As soon as your schedule begins to fill up, begin returning favors. Recommend your "gig angels" even when you're fairly sure that they're too busy to accept more work – it's the thought that counts.

Even your family can get into the act. They will probably not be able to get you a gig at Carnegie Hall, but they might know someone who's throwing a party.

Below is my list of **21 Job Ideas and Opportunities**. Some of them require further study or formal training; others you can try today. Read *Promote or Perish* in which I explain how to advertise your products and services. I discuss other methods of finding work throughout Part 3. Regardless of what kinds of gigs you get, or how you get them, you should always prepare, keep your ears and eyes open, and learn from your mistakes.

1) Street play. Don't judge this advice until you try it. Street playing is a quick, fun and easy way to generate income. If you're good – and pick a busy corner – you can make decent dinero. When I was 16, I bought the tenor saxophone I still use from money I made by playing on the street corners of Berkeley. Playing outdoors helps you develop your sound because you're forced to project it into open space while maintaining proper intonation and timbre. Plus you'll meet interesting and possibly helpful people.

2) Make a demo recording and give copies to anyone who will listen, particularly club and band managers, producers, contractors, and song writers. Inevitably, new technologies will make CDs obsolete; there are already plenty of options, like posting MP3s on your website.

But for now you're safe producing and distributing CDs. When you make any type of demo, follow the basic guidelines below, some of which are applicable to full-length CDs:

a) It should be under 5 minutes long.

b) Your best material should be at the beginning of your demo. If you've already played on a hit song or a familiar jingle, make it the first track.

c) Either exhibit one area of your playing or writing in which you excel, or demonstrate *all* your abilities. Each excerpt should last for 30 seconds or less.

d) Put your tracks in an order that will hold the listener's attention: consider the tempo, groove, instrumentation, and key of each candidate; keep it lively but put slower or more esoteric material in strategic places; include crossfades (blending the end of one track into the beginning of the next) if you have access to the necessary equipment; go for *flow*.

e) The production quality and volume should be consistent from track to track. Don't include low fidelity recordings even if you played brilliantly on them. Use only the best duplication equipment; if you hire a duplication service, know what machines they use and be very specific about EQ, compression, and volume levels. Make sure to ask the CD service to give you a sample CD, and to listen to it on several different systems before you authorize them to make more copies.

f) Whether or not you can afford expensive packaging, always be creative with the design; make it as fancy, funny or far out as you can. Hire a designer or ask an artist friend to assist you. Make sure that your contact information is legible and up-to-date.

(For more information on making a full-length CD, refer to *To Sign or Not To Sign*.)

3) Audition and sit in relentlessly. Even if you don't want the job, audition for it just to gain more experience and meet people. You can find audition notices on the Web, in the back of music trade papers, in the classified section of your local newspaper, and on college and union bulletin boards. When you speak with the audition organizer, ask her as many specific questions as she'll answer: what the job involves; which songs to learn; who will accompany you; who will preside over the audition; whether it will be filmed or recorded; what to wear; the number of people auditioning; whether non-musical skills will be considered. Sometimes you won't be given anything but a time and an address. Even if you do know all the details, it doesn't necessarily help to prepare beyond getting a good night's sleep. Still, a little information *can* go a long way. When you do an audition, arrive early, be friendly, do your best, leave promptly unless the audition coordinators ask you to stay, and forget about it the minute you walk out of the door.

4) Put a band together to play at weddings, hotel bars, bar mitzvahs, corporate parties, and industrial shows. Though I discuss various elements of band chemistry, etiquette, and promotion throughout this book, there are three essential requirements for building and maintaining a happy, healthy band that should be mentioned at the outset.

First, define your band's mission and your music; know your market, your audience and your limitations; don't try to be all things to all people. Second, whether your band is set up as a collective or as a benevolent dictatorship, communication is king: make sure that each member knows the band's "mission" and understands her own role, but feels that she can speak her mind and that her suggestions are taken seriously; build trust. Finally, nothing makes a band member more loyal and enthusiastic than abundant, lucrative gigs at primo venues. Keep your band in the black.

5) Put a band together to play at clubs and colleges. Remember that club owners and managers are primarily interested in selling drinks, and usually don't care what you play as long as you attract a crowd. You can buy a great deal of artistic freedom when you fill a room with free-spending friends and fans. Build a solid local following by sending regular e-mails to anyone who will sign your mailing list. Talk

about your band to everyone you meet. Give t-shirts and CDs to your faithful fans.

Avoid playing at one club too often, unless it results in a loyal and growing fan base. In general, spread your music far and wide: you will attract new fans, and your existing fans (and your band) will enjoy the variation in venues. When your band isn't working, stay in touch with your followers and let them know about your current recording activities and future plans. Thank them for their support.

Beware of "pay-to-play" deals, where you actually pay a fee to book your band at a club. This disease spread through the Los Angeles club scene in the early 1990s. Don't volunteer to be ripped off.

6) Promote yourself and your band in every way possible. If you're already well-connected and ready for prime-time, see if you can get someone from Creative Artists Agency (management) or Live Nation (promotion) to check out one of your live shows. Upload your best videos to YouTube. Paste the Web with your music.

7) Collaborate with as many people as you can. Two heads *are* better than one; even if you don't produce fabulous music or make buckets of cash together, you'll make new contacts via your colleagues.

8) Play union trust fund gigs. The AFM will provide you with the necessary information and forms.

9) Play at hospitals, nursing homes, and mental institutions via organizations like HAI (Hospital Audiences, Inc.: 212-575-7681).

10) Look in your local yellow pages for businesses that might use music. Call them and see if they can use your services. Here are several to try:

Adult Education Centers, Advertising – Radio and Television, Audio-Video Production Services, Bands and Orchestras, Banquet Halls, Bars and Grills, Cabarets, Cafes, Caterers, Cocktail Lounges, Community Centers, Convention Information Bureaus, Convention Centers, Country Clubs, Entertainers, Entertainment Bureaus, Dinner

Theaters, Fairs, Hotels, Motion Picture Studios, Music Arrangers and Composers, Music Producers, Musicians, Nursery Schools, Nursing Homes, Party Planners, Park Departments, Public Schools, Restaurants, Universities, Wedding Consultants, and Youth Services.

11) Though it's now a ridiculously crowded field in a deep recession, try to break into your local studio scene (see *So You Want To Be a Studio Musician*). Most of the record, film, and jingle work is still done in New York, Los Angeles, Nashville and Chicago, but there are thousands of small production houses scattered around the world which produce music for cable TV, Internet sites, cellphones, independent films, industrial shows, video and computer games, and other uses. Call them, visit them, give them your demo recording, and invite them to your gigs.

12) Give private lessons or teach at a school (see *So Much To Learn*).

13) Put together a home studio and sell services such as film scoring, CD duplication, song demo and voiceover production, sound design, and Pro-Tools editing.

14) Write music that kids and amateurs can easily sing or play, and produce songs for young artists.

15) Send a professionally produced video, 8 x 10 photo, and your résumé to all the casting agents in your area; you never know when a client will need a real musician (or your instrument) for a print ad, TV commercial or film.

16) Start a music preparation service. Most professional copyists now use computer software, but some clients prefer handmade charts.

17) Work at a music store – another way to meet people (and get equipment discounts). Learn instrument repair, and eventually start your own repair shop.

18) Run a rehearsal studio. With the right location, gear and advertising, your business will thrive.

19) Work on a cruise ship. Contact the biggest cruise lines first: two are Carnival and Royal Caribbean.

20) Become a music therapist. Even if you don't actually pursue a music therapy degree or a career in music therapy, it's a fascinating field, and all musicians benefit by learning something about it. If nothing else, it will enhance your communication skills.

21) Hang out with creative people – poets, painters, actors, dancers, designers and filmmakers. Jobs – or at least job ideas – will come your way.

Most of all, keep on plugging away with unyielding determination. Maintain high hopes and low expectations.

Rehearsal Blues

Being a bandleader and a sideman, I probably rehearse more than I sleep. Though the music, number of musicians, rehearsal spaces, rehearsal lengths, and expectations vary, a few rules are universal:

1) The musicians who "don't like to rehearse" are often the ones who *need* to rehearse.

2) Be on time. There's nothing more annoying than waiting for a colleague to show up when you'd rather be somewhere else.

3) Be prepared. Know the material. Bring everything required, and more. Be the one who everyone admires for having their act together and playing great.

4) Without a captain, the ship will run aground faster than you can say "shiver me timbers." *Someone* needs to crack the whip, or precious rehearsal time will deteriorate into yet another "hang." Yes it's fun to see everyone, but show up ready to work.

I've played hundreds of great gigs without rehearsing; some bands thrive on the spontaneity of hitting the bandstand cold. And the crazy schedules of most musicians – particularly the really good ones – make it tough to get everyone in the same city, let alone the same room. But I always prefer the luxury of rehearsing to achieve musical symbiosis, work stuff out, try new things, memorize songs, and cultivate deeper relationships with my peers. Just listen to a good orchestra to hear the results of regular, disciplined practice. Great things happen when talented, responsible musicians work towards a common goal.

Gimme My Money

Now that you've got a gig, there's the nagging little issue of compensation.

I've heard plenty of musicians say, "I don't like dealing with money. It just causes problems." It's when you *don't* deal with money that the problems begin. The more you "take care of business" the less you have to worry about it. Clear agreements are particularly important when you're working with friends, and with colleagues who don't like to talk about money. Bartering and asking for favors is fine, but make sure all parties are on the same page. It's common for "unspoken" agreements to sour when one party starts keeping score, or has the perception that the other party is doing so. And when more than two people are involved? Bandmates, ex-bandmates, composers, producers, managers, agents and roadies sue each other all the time – sometimes years after the alleged infractions. It's not surprising. Money is, after all, the root of all evil, and disputes over money are often the cause of divorces and band breakups.

When you're in a commercial jungle like the music business, you need all the help you can get, but choose your help carefully. Don't use lawyers therapeutically or to let off steam – they cost too much. Don't hire a manager or booking agent until you're too busy to handle your own affairs, until you have a product that justifies the expense of professional promotion, or unless you're hopelessly inept at business. Although "word of mouth" deals are the rule, try to get everything in writing. Don't pay to have your music sold on the Web unless you're absolutely certain that the company is effective, solvent, and makes timely royalty payments. CDBaby, Tunecore, and Reverbnation are good options. Make sure to register your original songs, arrangements, and recordings with the copyright office (call 202-707-3000 or go to copyright.gov for more information and to order the necessary forms).

One of the most important things you can do to protect yourself from the wolves, witches and goblins who populate our crazy little world is to join the American Federation of Musicians (AFM: 212-869-1330) via your local musicians' union. The union helps you in many ways: it sets and enforces minimum payment scales for all types of gigs; it collects and distributes session payments and residuals for recording work; it forces employers to pay you on time, and to give you a penalty fee if they pay late; it forces arbitration when unsolvable contract disputes arise; it enables you to participate in an excellent credit union that charges low fees, has low minimum account balance requirements, and offers low-interest loans. Moreover, the union runs effective assistance programs for substance abusers, and its trust fund sponsors live gigs around the country. Finally, it collects employer pension and health contributions on your behalf. As an illustration of the indispensable long arm of the union, I recently received a residual check for a TV show I'd played on in 1979. Since the show had only been running in the South, I would never have known that any back payments were due unless the AFM had been monitoring the contract.

While you're at it, join the Recording Musicians Association (RMA: 323-462-4762) which both assists and monitors the AFM, and presents your concerns to Congress and to the recording industry.

If your wages are not set and enforced by a union, you must jump over a formidable hurdle every time you get called for a job. Negotiation is a complex art that I won't discuss in depth here. But I've noticed that a) most musicians are not good businessmen, and b) $50 has been the typical non-union, under-the-table club pay for almost a century. Beyond these two limitations, the sky's the limit. Here are ten suggestions to get you started:

1) Read a good book on the art of negotiation, such as <u>*Getting to Yes:*</u> <u>*Negotiating Agreement without Giving In*</u> by Roger Fisher and William Ury, and <u>*Negotiating for Dummies*</u> by Michael C. Donaldson and Mimi Donaldson.

2) Find a few good lawyers, even if you don't need one right now.

3) Don't take business personally. And make sure you have friends outside the business.

4) Exercise sensitivity when you're negotiating with someone who's uncomfortable with or inept at talking about business. Be clear but gentle, and helpful but not condescending.

5) Find out *everything* about a gig – even if it's just a "quick hit" at some blues joint – before you negotiate or say "yes." What equipment do you have to bring? What are the *real* hours of employment? (Include time for transportation, including load-in and load-out, when you'll have to wait for the lighting truck to move.) Will you need to learn any material, and if so, how complex is it? I'm always amazed at how many employers misrepresent or omit the terms of a job. It will help down the line if you're thorough during your initial conversation with your prospective boss.

6) Always let the employer make the first offer. Sometimes it will be higher than you expected, and if it's not, you're in a better position to make a viable counteroffer. Be consistent, professional and persistent. Gain perspective by putting yourself in your opponent's shoes.

7) Some employers will ask you for favors, and some will not. Some employers will return those favors, and some are so cheap that they'll move on to their next "victim" rather than make good on their promise to "make it up to you when I get a better gig." You can't make a silk purse out of a lying, stealing, cheating scumbag. Give *everyone* a chance to do the right thing, and if they don't, move quickly to greener pastures.

8) Expect that you'll have many great gigs dangled in front of you, only to be snatched away for reasons beyond your control. Even if you're a bigwig, don't also expect that you'll be paid fairly (or anything) for canceled gigs that are not secured by a contract, or that you'll even receive a proper apology. Rug-pulling is a common practice in the music business. Try to fall gracefully, with dignity in tact.

9) You can charge more when you have a substantive track record.

10) Money talks. Money means nothing. Sorry, I haven't figured this one out yet.

Good luck, and don't tell them where you got the advice.

Taking Care of Business

Money, as Cyndi Lauper sang, changes everything. Never overestimate the value of money. Never underestimate the value of money. It's only money. I'm *still* working on that one.

Whether you play for a symphony or on the street, your income as a musician is relatively unpredictable. We do a little better on average than our actor, painter and poet brethren, but lucrative, steady work is often short-lived: Broadway shows and nightclubs close; tours end; musical tastes change; injuries occur; technology triumphs. It behooves you to be extremely cautious with whatever money you do make so that you can both invest in your career and save for the inevitable slumps. Don't develop a lifestyle that you can't sustain.

During flush times and bull markets you hear hyperbole such as, "It's not how much you spend – it's how much you make." Au contraire. Especially if you freelance, the key is disciplined saving, which requires disciplined spending regardless of how much you make. Think of it as paying yourself before you pay Ma Bell. Use your low-interest money market, savings or checking account to make automatic transfers to stock and bond mutual funds. The idea is to make fixed investments at regular intervals, and not to look at or touch the account as the stock market swings to and fro. It's called "dollar-cost-averaging" and you should research it further using a good financial guide like the _Wall St. Journal Lifetime Guide to Money_. You might be surprised to find out that if you put $100 per month into a conservative, diversified mutual fund yielding 8% per year, in ten years you'll have $18,295. Unfortunately, the recent market turmoil has frightened many people from saving and investing at all. Maintain a long-term perspective, and you will most likely prosper.

Another possibility for long-term savings is home ownership, as long as you avoid predatory lenders, draconian loan terms and high interest rates, and intend to stay put for awhile. Banks in several cities (e.g. New Orleans) have combined to create a home-ownership fund for local musicians and artists to help them buy or renovate homes, and there are many government-sponsored loans and tax breaks you can utilize. Though the current foreclosure rate is way up, and home prices are way down, don't throw in the towel. Again, think long-term: this could prove to be the best time to buy since the _last_ housing crash.

If you want your nest egg to grow fast, the best thing you can do is to save more money. Even if you can't bring yourself to learn a little about the stock, bond and real estate markets, and even if you don't have the discipline to stick to a monthly plan, it is imperative that you keep at least a six month cash cushion in your savings account. It will come in handy, particularly if you do a lot of seasonal work like weddings. Think not in terms of a rainy day, but of a rainy year or two.

Since I'm writing this in the 21st century, I probably don't need to tell you to buy some kind of computer (see _Man and Machine_ and _Out of Sight..._). Whether or not you can also afford an accountant, it's a good idea to use software like Quicken and Filemaker Pro, or a free online service such as Yodlee Money Center (yodlee.com) to help you track your finances, especially accounts receivable. This is particularly relevant if you compose or do residual-based session work: as you receive payments, you log the commercial titles, contract numbers, and cycle dates; if you hear a spot or a song airing and no checks arrive, you can quickly supply your union with the information they need to help you.

Finally, if you're a bandleader, jingle house owner, record company accountant, or someone who signs checks for any reason, pay your employees quickly and generously; it will come back to you in spades via your loyal, hardworking, flexible staff and the good word on the street.

And you thought all you needed to do was practice.....

The Dedication Factor

"A musician must make music, an artist must paint, a poet must write, if he is to be ultimately at peace with himself. What a man can be, he must be."

– Abraham Harold Maslow in *Motivation and Personality* (1954)

Indian sitarists and tabla players often study for twenty years or more before they allow themselves to perform in public. They must master approximately 360 "Talas" (rhythmic cycles) and hundreds of shorter rhythmic patterns, improvise well, know how to play at both breakneck and tortoise-slow tempos, be versed in all of the arts, and find the time to practice yoga and meditate. Sixteen-hour practice routines are common.

Similarly, mastering the technical and harmonic intricacies of jazz, Latin and classical music requires complete dedication and long hours of solitary practice. All serious musicians spend a great deal of time alone, are continually humbled by the music they are attempting to tame, and often don't pursue "normal" social and recreational activities. Though you may choose to focus on other musical areas – or develop less self-abusive practice habits – let these insanely devoted musicians energize you. Also look to other fields for inspiration, e.g. science, sports, and skilled manual labor. Dedication to craft is evident in all of these demanding fields.

One of the most disciplined people I've ever worked with was Rudy Johnson, a saxophonist who managed to practice six or seven hours a day *on the road* – a herculean feat. Whether we were waiting on the tarmac to board the tour plane, or passing time at a concert hall, there was Rudy – oblivious to the hubbub around him – practicing complex études and jazz licks. I don't know if he actually bribed the hotel concierges or if he was merely lucky, but he always found a quiet, isolated room in which to practice *after* our shows. Pat Metheny, Chick Corea and Sonny Rollins are other legendary "road-practice" addicts.

Thousands of über-successful show biz workaholics like Phil Collins, Sting, Madonna, and Prince, could have retired comfortably years ago, but chose to take the work ethic to new extremes. Have you ever heard of Tata Güines? If you're from Cuba you have. Güines, who died in 2008, was the most celebrated conguero in the world – and the quintessential alchemist of musical discipline. This guy was *all* music. Word has it that *he* played 24 hours a day!

It's easy to become lazy if you're making big bucks in the music business: "Why mess with success?" or "I play so many gigs that I don't need to practice." Ironically it is equally as tempting to slack off if you think you're a failure: "I practice all the time and I'm not getting any richer" or "I sound better when I don't practice." Stop making excuses and leave money out of it; play music for its own sake; realize your full potential because it will make you (and probably others) feel good; your practice habits should be as routine as eating or sleeping. Set lofty goals, because you will likely jump higher to attain them; even if you don't actually reach your intended target, you will have moved yourself in the right direction. Don't let money, success, or depression interfere with your healthy addiction to hard work and serious practicing. Note, however, that there will be days, even weeks where you get nowhere at all, or where you just can't find the time or energy to practice. And the practicing you do now might not result in any perceptible improvement in your playing for months. This is par for the course, and you should take it in stride.

Finally, when you practice don't give yourself a concert; you should work on what you *don't* know and continually challenge yourself with material that is slightly more advanced than what you can play now. I often remind my students that there's no shame in practicing a difficult musical passage, or even one measure, until it becomes easy.

This can sound like cats mating, but if your neighbors aren't complaining, something is amiss. Listen to recordings of your own playing with a critical ear, and assess where you need work. Don't bother to listen to that "perfect" solo for the tenth time, unless you desperately need an ego massage.

Playing music is like the playing the "game" of life: it's perpetually humbling and you can't "win." But the more you practice, the luckier you get.

You Call That Entertainment?

Starting about 1980 and continuing through the present, practitioners at the *top* of the gig pyramid raised their standards to pre-1960 levels: the stars and their bands are immaculate; clothes and accessories are elaborate and expensive; the choreography is sophisticated; no one talks on stage unless it's part of the show; entrances and exits are made quickly and with a flourish; hecklers and other problems that arise are usually handled with grace and dispatch. And *no one* yawns on stage, or drinks anything but designer water.

What's going on here? In a word, backlash. After a long decline, traditional showmanship and strict performance standards have returned with a vengeance to the top ranks. Conservative, fiscally responsible forces took over the music business after the excess of the 70s and paved the way for a new performance ethic; the love of loot replaced the love of sex, drugs, and rock and roll. PR departments worked hard to dupe the public into thinking that groups like Duran Duran were the next Beatles; in reality the music, fashion, language, and attitudes of the 60s and 70s were simply being neatly repackaged and sold back to the baby-boomers who had defined that era. As commercial success became the main goal, the starmaker machinery tightened its grip: more and more bands were created or strictly controlled by corporate entities who discouraged controversial behavior, spontaneity, and personal excess; the punks and sadists worked alongside the Christian rockers and Kenny G.; relatively polite, innocuous (though self-centered) attitudes became the norm.

Another reason that there are high, rigorously enforced stage standards in the upper echelons of the music business is that the bands and artists who can afford the best, *buy* the best: well-paid employees don't mind following orders and don't want to jeopardize their fat paychecks with irresponsible behavior; from the newest roadie to the choreographer, everyone knows and does their job well; expensive lighting systems, sets, stage clothes, buses and airplanes are treated with reverential respect; a business-as-usual, early-to-bed attitude dominates even the hottest rock tours; very few stars with staying power want to earn their own reality show.

But the "foot soldiers" – the majority of rank and file musicians – have yet to receive their marching orders.

Don't wait until you get the call for a big gig. Regardless of your artistic, political, economic, and religious orientation, you stand to gain by following a few codes of behavior that will ultimately free you to concentrate more effectively on your music. If you're a side musician, or have a local band, follow the rules listed below; they will help insure that your employers hire you in the future, and they enhance your reputation among your peers. If these incentives are not enough, follow them because your potential fans have shelled out their hard-earned cash to see a great show. You never know who will be in the audience; sometimes your destiny is sitting at the bar.

These are tall orders but follow them as best as you can:

1) Always be on time (see *Be On Time. This Means You*).

2) Before the gig, find out what clothes you should wear; wear them. If your employer says, "It doesn't matter," wear something great anyway.

3) Make sure your guest list is in order before you play. "Scenes" at the door during your performance are the ultimate bummer.

4) Maintain eye contact with the bandleader or the conductor at all times. Be aware.

5) If you have a complaint, talk about it *after* the gig, keep it to yourself, or quit.

6) Don't eat or drink onstage. If you *must* have a beverage, don't put it on amps or any other gear, and be sure to remove your glass from the stage when you finish the set. And don't drink too much, if anything, offstage.

7) Don't noodle during sound checks. Don't play or talk in between songs.

8) Always give 110% – musically and personally.

9) Avoid "auto-pilot"; stay awake and aware; enhance the big picture.

10) Be helpful. (See *Mr. Nice Guy*.)

11) Be polite on and offstage.

12) Tip the bartenders and waiters who served you.

13) Display a cheerful countenance even when you're unhappy. There's more than enough gloom and doom in the world, so regardless of how miserable you *think* you are, try to spread a little joy. Find *something* to be enthusiastic about.

If you still feel sorry for yourself, think of the legend of the Indian emperor Akbar and his court musician Naik Gopal: The emperor ordered his musician to sing *Raga Dipaka* (Song of the Earthen Lamp). Because it meant that he would be consumed by fire as soon as he finished the song, the musician begged to be excused from this duty, but the emperor insisted. Hoping to escape his fate, the musician immersed himself in the river Jumna and began singing. When the water began to boil, he pleaded with the emperor to help him, but the ruler refused because he wanted to see evidence of the power of music. The musician burst into flames and his ashes floated down the river.

14) Avoid arrogance. Be confident, but not bossy. Certainly a bit of egoism, bravado, and good showmanship are part of your job description. But don't be a braggart or a highfalutin windbag (see *Be You Ever So Humble*).

15) Avoid a "locker room" mentality. This is particularly offensive to any women in the band (and sometimes in the audience), and can destroy the more focused energy required to produce an effective ensemble sound. If you must treat music as a sport, think baseball: this highly unpredictable game is usually played by disciplined, patient, well-paid specialists working towards a common goal – on the road. Sound familiar?

16) When the set is over, pack up your equipment immediately, and get out of the way. Show respect for the stage crew and the band that's playing after you.

17) Unless you're leading or co-leading a band, or making your own recording, you're part of someone else's masterpiece. Do the best you can, and then forget about it. Let go of "your" work – it was never really *yours* in the first place.

18) If the general MO in a band is mellow and/or conducive to experimentation, don't be a party pooper. Loosen up; chill out. Or go play with the square pegs. Conversely, if you're a half-shaven scrimshanker doing a conservative gig, get with the program. The bandstand is not the place to test your philosophy of life.

If you're a bandleader, follow these rules too:

1) Establish a relationship with the sound person and maintain eye contact with him.

2) Write a legible set list and give copies of it to all your band members. Include song keys, solo orders, and any other relevant information. Give copies to everyone in the band. If you're just "calling tunes," call them loud and clear and make sure everyone is paying attention.

3) Start the set on time. Do you know where your children are? 15 minutes before the set, check to make sure your bass player isn't on the bathroom floor. If you're sharing the bill with other bands and there are delays or cancellations which require you to change the length or start time of your set, stay flexible. Remain calm. Work with the authorities towards a constructive compromise. The bandleader (and band) who copes gracefully with scheduling "crises" and other unpleasant realities will be invited back.

4) Don't use sign language or hieroglyphics when you count the song off.

5) Talking to the audience is good. Talking to the audience too much is bad. Use your good judgment.

6) Either completely ignore hecklers, or drown them with love – make them part of the act. Also, get the rest of the audience to help: often they will take care of the problem for you. If none of that works, ask the manager, bouncer, or security team to deal with it (see *They Love Me, They Love Me Not*).

7) Even if your wife left you, your van broke down on the way to the gig, and someone swipes your iPhone, don't take out your problems on the audience – or on the band. Don't let them see you in a kerfuffle.

8) Be somewhat tolerant of your sidemen's personal problems. Forgive them for their musical faux pas, their creative lulls, and their goofy shoes. Or fire them.

9) When there's a musical "deviation," go with it. Try to make it sound intentional.

10) Always be prepared for disaster; Murphy's law was written for musicians. Bring the directions to and phone number of the gig site; carry extra batteries, strings, reeds, screwdrivers, flashlights, cables, adaptors, microphones, microphone clips, music stands, etc.; bring a list of potential subs for every musician in your band, and be sure to

include their phone numbers; remember to recharge your cellphone before the gig; remember to bring any contracts or employee forms; reconfirm the deal you have with your employer *before the job*. And if you hitch a ride with your drummer, wear a helmet in addition to wearing your seat belt – drummers love to stomp on pedals!

11) Respect your employees, and pay them well.

12) Take responsibility for everything that happens. That's why you're making the big bucks …

13) Try to have a good time regardless of what goes wrong. Don't sweat the small stuff. Usually, this will help your audience to enjoy the music.

Now all you have to do is play great, original music.

Mr. Nice Guy

In any group of musicians, there's at least one weak link. Maybe it's you. Maybe it *was* you, and now you're the head cheese. When I first got to New York, I found myself in situations where I was in over my head. There were certain music industry veterans who were kind and helpful to me when I needed it most, and others who were cold and condescending. I'm pleased to have been able to return some of the favors bestowed upon me in those early, difficult years. And as for the naysayers and impatient jerks, let's just say that in the immortal words of Sam Theard via Louis Armstrong, "I'll be glad when you're dead you rascal you."

Attempt to bring out the best in all the musicians you encounter, whether you like them as people or not; the music will sound better and you'll work more often. If one of your bandmates is lost – or isn't ready for prime time – offer to help. Determine whether you need to be direct and brief (explaining a specific musical phrase during a recording session), or more subtle (listening to someone kvetch).

The advice you give won't always be appreciated, but try anyway. Or just listen. Often when one of your co-workers is struggling it's because he's having health or family problems, or a bad day. Have mercy. If you're leading a band or a session and encounter a rabble-rouser who doesn't take kindly to hints, offer to pay him to leave – quietly.

Whether you're a ten-year-old violist in a school orchestra or the concertmaster of the New York Philharmonic, it's a good idea to treat all your colleagues with respect. It's the right thing to do, and there's no telling who will end up on the top of the heap.

The Musician's Best Friends

I'm talking about engineers, of course. And assistant engineers. You'll find them in recording studios, clubs and concert halls. Sometimes they're deaf and sometimes they're Dutch. Treat them all well – very well: know their names; know their kids' names; buy them birthday presents; recommend them for jobs; be patient with them during sound checks; never *actually* complain to them about anything; put them in your will.

The same applies to secretaries, roadies, production assistants, gofers, and every fan that takes the time to listen to you.

Just Say No Thank You

Though you should try to work in as many contexts as possible and remain humble, helpful, and high-minded when you're on the job, you should also know when to quit or when to say "no" to a job offer. It's unhealthy to stay on a gig that makes you bitter, and even worse if you take out your frustrations on the music. Of course, economic necessity can force you to put up with inferior working conditions. And everyone has their own threshold of pain. But you can cut your losses by being selective. You will get better jobs if you don't waste your creative resources and your positive energy on junk.

Low pay, long hours, excessive travel time, substandard accommodations, nefarious bandleaders, bad music, and lousy musicians are common "occupational hazards" that might make you want to leave a job or to decline work. Occasionally you'll have to play with colleagues who are superb musicians, but who lack social skills. Ignore them: they might need help, and you're probably not a trained psychologist. It's also likely that at some point you will experience a personality conflict with a band member that will develop into a full-fledged battle. Some musicians are born troublemakers. Try not to take their bait, especially while you're on stage. Know that there are friendships and mysterious alliances between bandleaders and band members that affect every aspect of *your* role in a band. These relationships won't disappear just because they make you uncomfortable, or because you play well. Either put up or get out, but always take the high road. If you decide to leave or refuse a job, it's usually not necessary to slam your employer or to burden him with the gory details of your dissatisfaction. Bow out gracefully: bridges are highly flammable.

Perhaps the best advice I can give you is to prepare for the worst on all the gigs that you accept. You will usually be pleasantly surprised.

Man and Machine

Smartphones and ProTools and Web! Lions and Tigers and Bears! It's OK, Dorothy. Technology won't hurt you. But you must not remain in the path of the steamroller – drive it! Do not a Luddite be.

The people who rail against technological advances are usually the first to be replaced by them. Technology triumphs – or is given an ample chance to win – if it results in a more efficient, cost-effective or simply useful product. This is as true of musical instruments as it is of cars. When the pianoforte was introduced around 1710, many of the harpsichord players of the day panicked, claiming that the end of music was at hand. Though the piano is now ubiquitous, music is alive and well, and there are still plenty of harpsichord players. Player pianos created another uproar. Similarly, when music first hit the radio, some musicians thought that club work would disappear, and record companies believed that record sales would suffer. Instead, live *and* recorded music flourished like never before. After the drum machine craze of the 1980s, there was an enormous creative backlash, and drummers were in demand again until sampled drum loops began to dominate. But there again, the drummers who mastered drum machines, triggered samples with pads, and learned to play *with* loops or even imitate them, got more work than ever.

Evidence of the universality and cyclical nature of technology can be found everywhere. Here is an excerpt from an article entitled "A Year After the Peak" (*Wall Street Journal*, March 2, 2001):

"The current technology boom and bust, it turns out, is nothing new. It's simply the latest in a long history of investment bubbles that have plagued shareholders since investing began. From the Dutch tulip bulb craze of the 17th century, to the locomotive revolution of the 19th, to the rise, fall and resurrection of personal-computer stocks and biotechnology stocks in the 1980s and 1990s investors have fallen madly in love with – and then madly out of love with – the hot technology of the moment."

It's true that music employers are divided into two main camps: those who use machines to replace musicians and save money, and those who know that when they hire a real bassist, saxophonist or keyboardist, they are hiring the *mind* of the musician in addition to his sound. Note that I include keyboardists; add synthesizer programmers, sample wizards, and DJs too. Computer-generated music can be as expressive or moving as any other kind, as long as there are talented people running the computers. Some musicians, musicologists, critics, and even certain factions in the musician's union think that they've identified the enemy in the new machines – that digital music is inherently evil. But art lives inside an artist's head, and the tools with which he chooses to convey that art are irrelevant. Samplers and their digital companions are simply a new family of instruments, like woodwinds and strings, with their own sonic possibilities that must be explored and mastered. At their best, they provide musicians and composers with a large, malleable sound palette to-go. The rest is up to the musician.

In my opinion, the best composers, orchestrators and producers have always been Solomon-like: they use the best musicians in tandem with the best machines. Until a machine can make truly great music without a musician at the helm, musical creativity and musicians are no more in danger of extinction than they were when the Victrola was introduced. There is beauty in flaw, and a computer programmer interpreting a violin can be as flawed (or as spontaneous) as a violinist interpreting Bach. I think musicians and composers will always find work because of their knowledge, unpredictability and ability to interact intuitively with other musicians.

Technology has given musicians, programmers and producers another choice: whether or not to work *alone*. Although you can write, play and produce valid and sometimes great music all by yourself, it's a shame if you don't at least experience the thrill of playing in a group. Many young musicians have missed out on the power and joy of collective brainstorming and spontaneous communal creation, and this is potentially tragic: most musical loners suffer from a spiritual isolation that is reflected in their music. At the risk of sounding like an old fuddy-duddy, I believe that at its best, making music is a social, real time experience; two heads are usually better than one. One-man bands rarely find their way out of the mental and sonic vacuums they create by working in solitary confinement.

And what about the devaluation of intellectual property and the dethroning of the artist as a cultural hero? Again, none of this is new – and no one has written the end of the story. I know, I know. MTV killed the radio star, and as for Napster ... remember all the hubbub? (see *To Sign or Not To Sign*). But don't shoot the messenger. Napster, Gnutella – and every other Internet music service that attempted to deny royalty payments to songwriters – were the inevitable result of copyright law trailing technological innovation; *the law will always lag behind the laboratory*. In addition, there's a misplaced sense of entitlement prevalent in the current generation – kids expect free music. To be fair, after years of paying $17 for CDs containing only three good songs, consumers have a right to be pissed off. Throw in a few wealthy pop stars who can afford to give away their music, and legions of people like us who just want to be heard, and – voilà! – Napster.

If you're a Web-music detractor, base your argument solely on the 3 Cs: Consent, Creative Control, and Compensation; the people who make music must a) be the only ones who can legally consent to give their music away, b) control how it's used, and c) be properly compensated for their work. Fighting the technology itself is a losing battle; modern, well-enforced international copyright laws are the only viable protection for intellectual property.

All new technology experiences growing pains. The infancy of e-commerce was remarkably similar to that of radio advertising. In fact, radio itself was first called the "World-Wide Wireless," – the original WWW. RCA filled its coffers by selling radios; advertising revenue was many years away. The remaining major record companies are beginning to offer cable-style monthly subscription services for music downloads – unthinkable just a few years ago. (See *Out of Sight* and *To Sign or Not To Sign* for more information on utilizing the Web.)

I'm not suggesting that all change is good; some things are better left alone. But you should learn to recognize and welcome positive change. For instance, if you're a senior citizen, you're probably dependent on technology even if you don't want to be. But there are several reasons that you should learn more about computers, music software, samplers, and synthesizers: developing any new skill is mentally stimulating; you might discover a new source of income in your retirement; you will bridge one of the gaps between you and your younger colleagues; modern music machines and the Internet enable you work with a colleague at home – sitting down. The Sinatra Channel on Serious XM Satellite Radio is a good thing too. Due to the lightening pace at which technology advances, the longer you procrastinate, the more daunting it will seem. Mind you, I'm no expert on machines: I'm still overwhelmed by the endless possibilities of the latest sound-editing software. I admit that sometimes keyboards make me crave the "simplicity" of my piano. However, owning a home studio, computer-based recording system – or even one good microphone – opens new sonic doors. Here are some devices to explore and methods to try, regardless of your age or level of expertise:

1) Don't bother to buy any fancy gizmos until you know how to make listenable recordings with a simple multitrack recording device, or computer program. Then, if you don't already own a home studio, start putting one together. There has never been a better time to buy; there's a continuing trend towards higher quality and lower prices for electronic equipment. Internet sales have reinforced this trend. If you're intimidated by or can't afford the luxury of buying a fast computer, the latest software, a top-of-the-line digital recording system, samplers, outboard gear, microphones, and speakers, you can still greatly benefit by getting *something* down on tape when the Muse visits. Just buy or borrow an inexpensive but well-made digital recording machine, preferably one with built-in effects and EQ, and get your feet wet.

2) If you play a portable instrument, at least buy a top-notch microphone (and/or amp) to supplement those that you find in clubs and studios. If you're a horn player or vocalist, check out the latest wireless systems; most of the inherent problems – feedback, interference, etc. – have been addressed.

3) Put together a portable rack containing your favorite reverbs, compressors, samplers, and an analog-to-digital converter to enhance your live sound, or buy one multi-effects unit. Thrill the audience with your sonic magic.

4) Learn a software notation program. I know many musicians who make a good living moonlighting as computer copyists.

5) Smartphones and other hand-held computers, MP3 players, cable modems, T-3 lines, wireless Web services – these were *made* for musicians. Buy all of them if you can. The investment can pay off.

6) Talk with engineers and other knowledgeable sonic sorcerers. Ask a lot of questions, and write down the answers.

7) Read websites, books and magazines that discuss music and sound technology, and review new products. Also, make sure to read your

equipment manuals thoroughly; mastering one machine will make learning other machines easier.

If you don't want or can't afford to buy any new gear, at least learn about it so you can have intelligent conversations with your colleagues, and hold your own at sound checks and in modern studios. Master technology lest it pass you by.

PART 2:
THE NEXT PLATEAU

How to become a better musician.

Know Thyself

Developing a mature and recognizable musical personality usually takes many years. Regardless of whether you're just spreading your wings or making your seventeenth hit record, try to feature what is unique about your playing when you rehearse, record or perform live. Satisfying yourself, pleasing the bandleader, and thrilling the audience are not mutually exclusive activities.

But can you accurately evaluate your own abilities? It might help to talk with your friends and colleagues. Pick direct, sincere people – you're not looking to be stroked. Buy your confidant a beer and ask, "What would you say are my main strengths and weaknesses as a musician?" I guarantee that if you pose this question to a wide variety of people you'll get a fairly accurate idea of how you're perceived – the whole enchilada in the music *business*.

Display your musical strengths on stage and in the studio and work on your weaknesses elsewhere. For instance, if you have a good sound, make it even better: talk with engineers and learn all you can about microphones, pre-amps, boards, compressors, effects, and acoustics; make sure your instrument is in top condition; improve your tone in the upper and lower extremities of the instrument and at all volumes; work on maintaining the tone quality when you apply various articulations. Then, when you perform, play some long notes and let everyone hear that gorgeous sound.

Most producers, arrangers, composers and bandleaders expect their sidemen to be able to both "read the ink," and add tasteful embellishments on demand. Learn to interpret music in your own way; a spontaneous grace note or fall-off can make the difference between a flat performance and a dynamic one. If the gig or rehearsal you're doing allows even a little creative latitude, ask your boss for a chance to enhance the written music. Try leaving a note out here and there, adding a run or a turn, playing something in a different octave, momentarily changing the feel, growling – anything that makes the music *speak*. If your employer hates what he hears, he'll let you know and you can humbly saunter back to your corner and play the unadorned chart.

Ideally, your music is simply an extension of your personality and your imagination. Once you've removed as many technical barriers as possible, you can play straight from the heart. Hopefully you'll get more gigs where being yourself is the whole point.

To Thine Own Self Be True

I have no patience for the reconstituted Michael Brecker solos that are mindlessly spewed forth by legions of pseudo-jazz-brat automatons, not to mention the rampant Sanbornification prevalent in many young saxophonists. Since imitation is the sincerest form of flattery, we need a law that limits how long a musician can flatter one mentor. But you've got to start somewhere; steal some seeds first, blossom later.

When I was sixteen I was cribbing every Brecker and Sanborn solo I could get my hands on. But I was also smitten with Joe Henderson, Dexter Gordon, Sidney Bechet, Ornette Coleman, Lester Young, Coleman Hawkins, Rahsaan Roland Kirk, Junior Walker, Johnny Hodges, John Coltrane, Stan Getz, Flip Phillips, Wayne Shorter, Jan Garbarek, Sam Butera, Cannonball Adderley, Dewey Redman, Pharoah Sanders, Sonny Rollins, Illinois Jaquet, Eddie Harris, Oliver Lake, Gene Ammons, Chu Berry, Charlie Parker, Ernie Krivda, Eric Dolphy, Johnny Griffin, Paul Desmond, Ben Webster, Yusef Lateef, and dozens of other superb musicians.

Somewhere along the way I discovered my own voice. I know that my main strengths are in my passionate sound, my humor, and my choices of what *not* to play; I'm there to serve the *song*. When I do studio work I can draw on the vast stylistic repertoire I developed years ago when necessary. Jan Garbarek? No problem. I'm nuts about his playing. But I'll never understand why anyone would want to make him their *sole* musical reference. Certainly when a song requires that you play in a certain style you do it, even if it means imitating a musician you *dislike*. Sometimes interpretation or innovation isn't part of the job description. And it never hurts to study and pay homage to your mentors. But be a sponge – not a clone.

Originality (or at least the occasional good idea) is particularly important given the glut of the current music marketplace. If you're in a band, help to break through the status quo by striving for your own sound. So many bands sound alike that it's almost easy to stand out. Just play with dynamics and you will amaze your audience! If you choose to merely copy an existing model, you'll sound generic and cheap; stay off this ferris wheel of plagiaristic bad taste unless you're playing in a tribute band, hotel or industrial cover band or a no-frills wedding band. It's true that every time a record company scores a big hit, their competitors scramble to find a clone of the hit maker; many bands get signed *because* they sound like someone else. But these second-hand bands rarely make second records. Once that "new" sound falls out of favor, the label heads want to hear the *next* big thing. Lead the way.

It is said that nine-tenths of originality is bad memory – and nine-tenths of genius is hard work. I'd put it in another way: originality is partly a creative synthesis of the best in classic work. And true genius is so rare, we'll never truly understand it. Know the traditions from which you draw and combine the elements of sound, rhythm, harmony, phrasing, emotional intent and technique in innovative ways and thereby find your own voice. When you cultivate your own musical identity, you'll sleep better at night and stand a better chance of having a long, satisfying and potentially lucrative career.

Beyond the Notes

Your prowess as an instrumentalist means precious little if you're not also a good musician. Beyond articulation, phrasing, dynamics, and an innate sense of swing lies the rarefied realm of sonic poetry – of unadulterated soul. To get there you need to live a little, play with and listen to superior musicians, and perhaps most important, absorb the techniques of the master vocalists. These modern minstrels are part of a glorious storytelling tradition dating back thousands of years. Whether you're a Baroque harpsichordist or New Age tuba player, you can learn something from archetypical soulmasters like Ray Charles, Stevie Wonder, Neil Young, Bob Marley, John Lennon, Mildred Bailey,

Frank Sinatra, Patsy Cline, Taj Mahal, Bessie Smith, Johnny Cash, Muddy Waters, Billy Holiday, Milton Nascimento, Bob Dylan, Louis Armstrong, Joni Mitchell, and Al Green. Some of these folks needed to dig particularly deep because of their technical limitations; all of them are in tune with the collective human spirit. Imitate any singer who moves you. If you really want to learn how to tell a story, listen to country, bluegrass, and folk music from around the world. Charlie Parker did.

Always think like a singer: practice playing a full range of vocal-like nuances on one note at a time; abandon "correct" tone production techniques, and see if you can produce sounds not usually associated with your instrument; mentally eliminate the hunk of metal or wood in your hands, and pretend that you *are* singing. Of course when you play live, not all of these tonal subtleties will exhilarate the audience or hold universal appeal. But half the battle of musicality is won by "singing" every time you play. Also imitate sounds from nature and from machines – every sound you hear. The more sounds you add to your tonal arsenal, and the more chances you take, the more you will move beyond mere notes.

Great music has a supernatural quality about it that transcends mere technical or intellectual prowess. We know that our emotions, our spontaneity, and our capacity for nuance all play a significant role, but it's possible that God, ESP, or the spirit world are there to help us too. The point is, you should "get out of the way" to make room for a visit from Beyond; once you've learned a piece of music or memorized a set of chord changes to improvise on, you must "lose" yourself in the music, and let it flow *through* you; just play. Sometimes the music itself is enough to get you to "stop thinking." On other occasions it may help you to "go someplace else" through visualization: think of shapes; colors; someone you love; space, the beach; Italy; nothing. Don't hesitate to explore the Land of Make-Believe. The games you played as a child were spawned by your unbridled imagination; the same wellspring of creativity can work wonders for you now.

Surely the quest to reach higher musical ground leads many musicians to experiment with drugs and drink, which in turn deadens the spirit and potentially kills the experimenter. Instead, use more powerful resources: your heart and your soul. Free your mind and the rest will follow.

I Can't Go On . . .

Stage fright. If you've never had it, you're lucky. Or maybe not. At this point in my career I welcome that freaky feeling, because I know how to channel my excess energy into a better performance. It can be motivating to be nervous. Things always seem to calm down after the first song or two anyway.

For some people, though, stage fright is debilitating. Carly Simon, even after a string of pop hits, waged a war with the pre-show jitters that took years to win. My mother played violin as a kid and said that she was a wreck before, during, and after her performances. Assuming you're a full-time musician, and you have similar difficulties, you should seek professional assistance. Otherwise, try performing *more*.

For me, playing in front of thirty thousand people is much less nerve-racking than playing in a small club when the audience is sitting and listening carefully. My hands even sweat a little when I play for my family. Large crowds are a faceless sea of energy which is easy to ignore; sometimes you look out and all you can see is lights. Either way, I usually close my eyes when I play, since it helps me concentrate on sound.

Many performers who experience stage fright are perfectionists, or at least hard on themselves. If you fit into this category, try to lighten up. It's only music; wrong notes don't spell the end of the world. Experiment and discover the little tricks that will make it better for you personally, like taking a walk around the block or eating a doughnut before you play. Some of my colleagues report that they talk to friends who make them laugh or calm them down before they perform. Find a comforting routine, something simple and repetitive.

Everyone handles stage fright in a different way. Anxiety in medium doses is essential for *any* achievement, whatever the profession; it motivates sustained effort and focuses your attention. Lack of tension can diminish your creative output; too much tension can cause mental paralysis. We all have a mental "center" – a place where we can enjoy the moment and get on with the work at hand. Find yours.

Are We Having Fun Yet?

Musicians tend to take themselves and their music much too seriously. I'm certain that this results from the tedious hours of solitary practice and rehearsal required to achieve excellence. And there's nothing funny about repetitive stress injuries, erratic schedules, and intermittent unemployment. It's easy to forget the joy that you experienced when you first discovered that you could extract mellifluous sonorities from a hunk of metal or wood.

But do you want to play music made for the musicians, or for the people? There is a difference. Figure out whether you're an artiste, an entertainer, or a combination of the two. If the former applies, I suppose that you have the right to display a weighty countenance, and to never let your music smile. But if you feel any obligation to your audience, embrace humor with open arms.

There are many ways you can tickle the listener: if you're improvising, quote from a comical, witty or lyrically relevant song; bend, flutter-tongue, growl, or squash a note or two; simulate a conversation by answering yourself in different registers of your instrument; conjure a bit of Sturm und Drang; play as if you're smashed. Listen to the soundtracks of old sitcoms, and the kitschy lounge music from the 50s and 60s. Draw on the brilliant musical comedy of artists like Louis Jordan, Noel Coward, The Marx Brothers, Mel Brooks, Monty Python, the Second City folks ... and study cartoon music. In particular, check out Carl Stalling's superb music for Warner Brothers' Loony Toons.

When musical jests are inappropriate, it becomes even more important to give the crowd *something* to lift their spirits. Enter physical humor – particularly important for classical musicians. Ever watch Yo-Yo Ma? Now *he* has a good time. Is it the sheer delight of making his cello sing? Whatever it is, he's great to watch. Spirited camaraderie, intelligent parodies and puns, well-placed gestures and funny faces delight audiences. And though some fans only come for the music, the majority of any audience wants you to talk to them. Great bandleaders know that they must perfect an informative, flowing style of between-song patter – also a great time to tell an anecdote or a joke. Go hear Jonatha Brooke, Tom Waits, and Keb Mo – they've got it down. The Three Tenors came up with a knee-slapper now and then. Dizzy Gillespie co-invented bebop, ran for president, and always made his audiences laugh.

Of course clowning can easily go too far and ultimately diminish the overall effect of the music: like every trick it should be used in moderation, if not sparingly. Not everyone is naturally funny and no one can fake esprit; most of the time, funny simply happens. Goofiness is particularly nauseating when it is substituted for musical substance. Just try not to be morose, unless that's your entire schtick and everyone gets it.

Simple joie de vivre will do. As Charlie Chaplin wrote, "You'll find that life is still worthwhile, if you just smile."

Space is the Place

The notes you do not play are more important than those you do. Though this is ubiquitous and excellent advice, it is often ignored in the heat of the moment. How tempting it is to play everything you know, and to play it too quickly, as if there were no tomorrow. But even if you're humble by nature, it will look as if you're showing off.

Listen to Miles Davis records. Listen to the spaces he leaves in his solos. Even when he plays at lightning tempos, you hear the spaces. More often than not he says more with one note than most say with fifty. Don't forget Thelonious Monk and Count Basie. And check out Aretha Franklin: *she's* got the world – and the heavens – wrapped up in every note, and doesn't need to sing too many to get her heart heard.

Unless you're in an orchestra, or play improvised instrumental music full time, you'll probably work frequently behind singers, or on sessions where a voiceover is the main focus. This requires diligent sensitivity and shrewd note selection. You're there to embellish the lyrics – to make the vocalist shine – and you should pay strict attention to the song's ebb and flow, to its total intention. The fills and solos you play must be idiomatically correct, and your tone should compliment the voice. Make every note count. Most important, listen to what's already there – sometimes the music is busy enough.

Listen to David Sanborn playing behind James Taylor (or any singer), Lester Young with Billy Holiday, Stan Getz with Astrud Gilberto, and Jerry Douglas with Alison Kraus. You will notice a profound difference between their approaches to vocal versus instrumental music. These cats know the lyrics inside and out. They never play unnecessary notes. And they *never upstage the singer*.

Style-Hopping

In contrast to most modern physicians, the modern musician is less specialized. The proliferation of music on the Internet has reinforced this trend because everyone everywhere hears everything. Studio, Broadway, and clubdate/casual musicians have always had to master multiple styles and many bandleaders demand tremendous versatility from their backup musicians. There are still plenty of clarinet players who live for Polka music, but they're probably thinking about branching out. As I mentioned above, you should know your strengths and seek your own musical identity. But your musical palette and your marketability will be greatly enhanced if you're at least familiar with music from many cultures, past and present.

Musicians are notoriously opinionated about what they hear – occasionally because they have discriminating taste, frequently out of ignorance. I know too many "jazz musicians" who hate rock, and coincidentally, can't play it to save their lives. I'm not suggesting that you can be all things to all people; especially when you make your own record, a narrow focus helps. But the well-rounded musician *listens* to everything. *Who* is playing is more important than the type of music being played. And each musical form requires slightly different "ear criteria"; you won't appreciate Nine Inch Nails if you're expecting to hear riveting acoustic bass solos.

Often one must study a musical genre in order to appreciate it, and this takes more time than most people have; think of how few Americans comprehend jazz. You must be more thorough than your audience: read music history; talk to club owners, producers, engineers, DJs, students, and fans about what they listen to; utilize the Internet to hear music from all over the world. You'll be surprised at what you don't know.

I frequently hear friends and colleagues complain about the dearth of great music on the radio and in the record store. What planet are they referring to? I don't even have time to keep up with all the great stuff in my own collection, or on satellite radio and the Web. I believe that there's an unwritten cultural and artistic "90/10" rule – that 90 percent of all art is merely OK, functional or utterly pathetic, that 10 percent is either good or magnificent, and that this ratio has been maintained since the beginning of time. The only fundamental differences between the present and the past are that everything moves faster now and, more important, that there's much more to choose from; sorting through the rabble to get to the crème de la crème can be a challenge. One more thing: a great deal of today's music is so unashamedly derivative that it takes disciplined research to uncover its superior source(s) of inspiration.

But regardless of the musical quality, find the intrinsic value in every recording or performance. Does one musician stand out as being superior? Does it swing even if the melody doesn't ring your bell? If the music stinks, how about the lyrics? Is there anything you can learn from the arrangement? From the production? If nothing else, does it remind you of something else you should hear? Great music sounds *inevitable*. Listen for this inevitability before you fulminate against a repetitive R&B groove or lambaste the simplicity of a heavy metal chord progression.

Following are seven simple but important reminders:

1) Do not confuse "don't like" with "can't do." If you don't know it, learn it. At minimum, understand it.

2) The song *rules*.

3) It's never all about you; even if you wrote the song, you are a cog, albeit an important cog, in the wheel. So make sure you're working

constructively with the other cogs. Defer to and learn from colleagues, bosses, and employees who know more than you about a particular musical style. Or go to your room (and work alone).

4) Know the role of every instrument in various contexts.

5) If you find yourself playing music you don't understand intellectually or viscerally, or if you're simply not playing well, stop thinking! Consult the vast void of your subconscious; play from the heart; stretch, meditate, go outside – do anything to get off of the cerebral hamster wheel.

6) When you style-hop, *be* the music: copy the attitude, pace, language, clothes, and dance styles of the best musicians and singers who define the genre; try to play only what is specific to the musical idiom; when you play the blues, do as the blues men do.

7) "Avant-garde" music becomes "cutting-edge" music which becomes "normal" music faster than you can say "Igor Stravinsky." Challenge your ears: draw inspiration from unconventional "new" music. Be all that you can be!

So You Want To Be a Studio Musician

Being a studio musician is much like being an actor: you must be able to play diverse roles under a variety of working conditions; you're often asked to sublimate your own artistic instincts to realize the vision of the director or writer; your patience will often be tested as hurry-up-and-wait is the rule; and being good at your craft doesn't guarantee employment or recognition. When everything is copacetic, you work short hours and get paid extremely well for making music with talented musicians, producers and composers. Occasionally you luck into playing on a hit album, film, TV show, or long-running jingle, and the dough rolls in for several years, or – once in a blue moon – for decades.

You must be prepared for anything. Each producer, contractor, conductor, arranger, writer, and recording artist has a unique way of getting the job done. Some of them will play reference material for you and ask you to sound as close to that recording as possible. Some write everything out; others assume that *you* will write or improvise the melody – a job that you should be compensated for. The definition of "in tune" may vary. One producer will demand clean, precise ensemble work; another will go for vibe before accuracy, or may even want you to play "badly" to achieve a certain effect. Sometimes you'll have to translate ridiculously vague or inarticulate verbal instructions into a perfect musical phrase that will help sell soap.

If you're lucky, you work for music bosses who know how to hire the right people for the job, who issue clear and concise instructions, who let the musicians work their magic, and who show their appreciation for a job well done. The less savvy ones either have no idea what they want, or much worse, assault you with conflicting instructions before you even begin, record twenty takes for no particular reason, and end up using your first take. This last scenario is all too common, and you should be prepared to let go of your "good" performances: beauty is in the ear of the "behearer."

You will make your life in the studio much easier if you're musically and personally flexible, listen carefully, react quickly, and humbly follow orders – even when you're being dragged down the garden path. The ability to concentrate under pressure is key. And the more styles of music you know, the better (see *Style-Hopping*). Here are some other things to expect when recording, and a few helpful hints which are also applicable to other musical situations:

1) One of the ancillary skills you must develop to be an effective studio musician is the ability to overdub a part on an existing rhythm track, and make it sound "live." The only way to master this skill is by doing it all the time. (It also helps to imagine that you're playing in a club.) You will also be asked to "play with yourself," i.e., overdub multiple parts to build a horn section, or to layer various percussion instruments. If you want this "one-man band" to sound natural, open those ears and listen hard! Think nuance: compliment the phrasing, dynamics, tone, and vibe of your first part.

2) You will often be required to replace a few notes or measures of a performance. Again, you must listen carefully to the notes you played before and after the "punch" points so you can match their rhythmic feel, tone, pitch and volume. It's also important that you maintain your position in relation to the microphone from take to take. With digital recording systems, producers have the luxury of keeping numerous tracks which can be edited together later. When you're asked to "replace" something that you like, just do it; the engineer is probably saving the original.

Conversely, when *you* hear something that you'd like to replace or add to, ask the producer to listen to that specific note or phrase. If he doesn't agree with you, *let it go immediately*. Sometimes it's more effective to use your hands to show the engineer or producer where the punch points are instead of using a description like "punch in on the third 16th note of beat 2 in bar 11 and punch out before beat 4 of bar 20." Occasionally you'll have to punch in one note or phrase over and over before you get it right. As always, patience is a supreme virtue, but if you reach the point of no return, ask if you can come back to that section later in the session.

3) Sometimes a producer will ask you to "add a few notes" or to improvise a 4-bar solo. At home, practice playing short "statements" or licks in a given musical style, or with a set of chord changes in mind. Use the limited rhythmic space wisely. In the studio, stay nimble of mind and finger as you may be required to play multiple versions of your solo for no apparent reason.

4) If you're recording a jingle, TV show, or a film, you might be asked to "play to picture" – to watch the screen for visual cues and translate them into musical ideas. This intuitive art was perfected by the musicians who accompanied silent films. The best way to improve your "sight to sound" translation skills (besides doing it a lot) is to improvise to television shows with the sound turned off. You might find you have a talent for writing film scores or video game music.

5) Only make musical suggestions when you're asked to give them. If you know your boss well you can usually express your unsolicited

opinion, but pick your battles carefully and always be the first to concede defeat. If you find yourself in a situation that cries out for your expertise, feel free but tread lightly – you're there to facilitate someone's artistic or commercial vision, and you're swimming amongst large yet fragile egos. Observing these protocols will be particularly easy if you've ever led a band or recorded your own material.

6) When the engineer checks your sound, play with the tone and the volume you'll be using for the track. If you accidentally change the position of your instrument or move the microphone during or between takes, make sure to tell the engineer.

7) Respect engineers and show your appreciation for their hard work – engineers are some of the most important people you will ever work with. They have their hands full and are invariably under more pressure than you are. Let the engineer make all of his adjustments *before* you ask him to do anything; he'll let you know when it's your turn to kvetch.

Headphone mixes (and headphones themselves) vary greatly. After you hear yourself in context, briefly describe what changes you want to make to your individual mix, if any. Be precise, as in "Bob, I need a little more of the bass and the lead vocal, and less snare drum," but don't bug him with minutiae. Also, if you're recording live with other musicians, there may be only one headphone mix available and you should consult your colleagues before you request any changes.

If an engineer uses a microphone, amplifier, effect or compressor that you don't like, and you have a viable alternative in mind, *politely* inquire as to the possibility of a switch. Keep in mind that some engineers believe that this is like asking you to use a different mouthpiece or string. Engineers can be touchy and you should avoid pissing them off.

8) Don't noodle between takes.

9) Turn off your cellphone, and any other audible devices.

10) Don't be too quick to turn up your headphones – your ears are precious and frail.

11) Assume that you'll be in the studio for longer than you planned. Sometimes you arrive only to learn that the session is running an hour or more behind and that your employer has only ten minutes to record your part. Occasionally you'll be there all day or all night. Learn to pace yourself: try to stay positive and relaxed; don't spend excess energy between takes by playing or yapping a lot, and try not to look at your watch or even think about the time. You must concentrate and stay completely focused on the work at hand, especially when you're enjoying yourself, or when the crew "behind the glass" is acting goofy. Bring something to read. Make sure to eat enough before you go to the studio, and maybe carry a snack and some water with you. An apple a day will keep vile sounds at bay.

12) Studio work is a minefield of potential problems: instruments break; machines fritz out; engineers erase great takes; copyists screw up; musicians have bad days or simply don't play well together; time and cash run short; sessions come up at the last minute and ruin your love life. And that's just for starters. Add in a few problems like bad music and 130 decibels of sudden, high-pitched feedback, and you might as well work at the Marriott in Grand Forks. Just kidding. I love studio work and studio work has been very good to me, and the Marriott's not bad either. Just know that if you're going to be a studio musician, you need nerves of steel and much patience.

13) Always do your best work, even if you dislike the music (or your boss). You're only as good as your last recording session.

Be You Ever So Humble

OK. So you've just returned from a world tour with the pop diva du jour. Maybe there are a couple of dozen hit recording credits on your résumé. It's a warm Saturday afternoon in June and you're looking forward to playing softball with friends and spending your first Saturday night at home in over two months. The phone rings and the raspy voice of a very sick colleague asks you to sub for him tonight, deep in

South Jersey with a band neither of you have heard. Partly because this guy has helped you before, and partly because you feel guilty for even considering a night off, you put away your catcher's mitt and take out your tux.

The directions are wrong; the catering hall reeks of ammonia and broccoli; the band members are dull and sound like crap; the "bandwiches" are inedible; the bride, the groom, the maitre d', and the guests act like they're starring in a Godfather movie, but are merely ridiculous and rude; it's a non-union date, and you do overtime.

This, of course, is a test. If you came off like God's gift to rock & roll, you failed. If instead you were friendly and helpful on and off the stage, played contextually and learned a tune or two, you're a winner. Not an easy gig. But this is one of those precious reminders of where you came from. Remember when you were happy just to be on stage? And from a business perspective, do you remember where your professional network came from? Only back then, the jobs were worse and paid less. It never hurts to make sure you can still handle tough circumstances with tact.

One of the worst things you can do is to use your talent or your success as an excuse to be a jerk; bad behavior in the name of "art" is inexcusable. Plus, you probably don't know as much as you think you do. Just when you're sure that you've seen and done it all, fate shakes your tree and an apple falls on your head. If you're lucky, you'll make a monumental scientific discovery – or at least learn something new.

One Good Discipline Deserves Another

One of the most difficult challenges you will face is staying musically inspired throughout your entire life. Musicians often try to accomplish this by listening to records, going to concerts, or practicing. While those activities are useful, my favorite way to stimulate creative output is to do something non-musical. It is essential to sail out of Bassoon Bay towards the ocean of human experience.

Start with art: go to a museum and actually *read* the little plaques beneath the paintings; go to the library and check out a biography of the artist who rocks your world; read it; go to another museum the following week, and so on. If you hate Picasso, improve your chess game or learn a new computer program. Raise tropical fish. Learn to cook. Going for a walk or a bike ride in the park can help too: besides breaking the monotony and stimulating your endorphins, you bask in the unpredictable rhythms of nature, the first music on earth. Exercise to expel the copious amounts of second-hand smoke you absorb when you play at clubs. Space out. Let your imagination run wild.

When is the last time that you completely stopped playing and listening to music for a while? You should do this periodically, particularly if you work or practice a lot. If you desperately miss your instrument, so much the better. Your musical imagination will rekindle itself when you let it rest, and you'll find time for important people and activities you've neglected during your practicing, composing and gigging frenzies.

It is essential to remember that the richness of your musical vocabulary and your ability to use it effectively are enhanced by the depth of your life experience.

So Much To Learn

During your career you'll experience many technical glitches and creative nadirs. When you experience these setbacks, use the time to work on your weaknesses with a good teacher. Even if everything is A-OK, there's nothing like taking a lesson with a seasoned pro to spark your art. Raise the bar even higher by learning a new instrument: You will invigorate your musical vocabulary, gain a new perspective on sound, and become more employable. Find a good teacher to get you started.

Every teacher will give you a different gift. One of my early piano teachers, Julian White, brought the great composers to life for me and taught me how to play classical music with heart. He was also one of the funniest people I've ever met. During my early teens, saxophonist Steve Elson taught me to improvise and play jazz. Then he showed me how to avoid becoming a jazz snob – that there was a huge world of music to explore; that being a musician is a narrow enough highway without closing any lanes. And finally, there was Phil Hardymon, the biggest influence on my career after my family. Phil had worked as a trumpet player in New York in the 1950s until he lost a lung in a car accident. He moved to Berkeley and, along with Herb Wong and Dick Whittington, dedicated his whole life to raising music in the public schools to unprecedented levels of excellence. Suffice it to say that by the age of fifteen, we were performing at the Monterey Jazz Festival, winning every big band and small ensemble award in California and Nevada, performing our own music in and around San Francisco, and developing the technical and psychological skills necessary to survive the musician's life; Phil turned us into dedicated musicians with a sharp eye on reality; he treated us like adults, so we *played* like adults. Us alumni – including Peter Apfelbaum, Steven Bernstein, Benny Green, Craig Handy and Joshua Redman – are doing pretty well. Phil Hardymon was an extraordinary teacher.

If you're not blessed with an award-winning school music program, or if you can't afford equipment and lessons, swap ideas, methods, riffs, instruments, supplies, sheet music, and books with your peers. Just talking with a smart musician can work wonders. Take advantage of continuing education courses at your local college; many offer music courses at various times of the day and night. You're never too old to go back to school.

The well-rounded musician should also acquire students of his own. If you only have time for one pupil every two weeks, begin there. To teach is to learn. When you review your own early training and explain basic concepts in new ways you will challenge and stimulate yourself, not just your students. And there's nothing more rewarding than helping beginners and amateurs become full-fledged professionals. I feel fortunate that many of my students have gone on to do great things.

I've also worked extensively with both individuals and groups of people with various physical and mental impairments. You only need to see a severely-withdrawn autistic kid respond to the blues to appreciate the power of music. The abstract nature of music helps us reach mysterious recesses of the human brain in ways that mere science can't fully explain. How does music heal? Are these the same channels that are tapped when you listen to a song that inspires you to dance or cry? Or does simply participating in something weird and fun activate endorphins which momentarily distract the patient? I suspect that there are lasting benefits from the spontaneous synaptic connections triggered by music. When the student or patient is able to play an instrument, even a little, the benefits increase exponentially. Regardless of the details, I've found that using music to help people is deeply satisfying, and it forces me to use my *own* brain in new ways.

Hopefully you'll also have some students who outdo you in certain areas. I've had Eastern European students whose double and triple-tonguing (probably learned from playing Polkas and such) floored me. Sometimes my protégés surprise me with a new take on a tired subject. They *always* inspire me to practice. It's not difficult to find students. In fact, I've been teaching since I was fifteen. Back then, as now, most of my students came to me by word of mouth or approached me at gigs. But you can also try putting up a poster on the bulletin board at your local school, grocery store, community center, or gym. Websites like Craigslist charge little or nothing for a basic ad. Tell your friends and colleagues that you're looking for students, and perform at your local school.

The student/teacher relationship is a precious resource, and should be fully explored.

Sing, Sing, Sing

Learn to sing. Period. Singing will make you a better musician, and – if you have a decent voice – probably double your income.

Singing improves your playing in three distinct ways: first, you will discover your "true voice," which makes you aurally distinct. Imitate your own voice when you play your instrument; you will sound unlike other musicians who play the same ax (think of Louis Armstrong and Dizzy Gillespie: both played the way they sang). Second, your playing will become more confident; the rigors of disciplined singing will make playing your instrument seem easy. Finally, singing develops your "mind's ear" enabling you to "hear" the note before you play it. This is particularly useful when you improvise; most of the early jazz musicians felt that if it couldn't be sung, it wasn't worth playing. This approach resulted in melody-rich instrumental improvisations, something of a lost art.

If these artistic benefits don't get you crooning, perhaps a look at the bottom line will. Vocal recording sessions and television performances fall under the jurisdiction of either the Screen Actors Guild (SAG) or the American Federation of Television and Radio Artists (AFTRA), two extremely powerful unions. As I mentioned previously, you should definitely join the AFM. But know that if you're lucky enough to *sing* on a jingle, SAG or AFTRA will collect a royalty for you *every time the jingle airs*, whereas when you *play* on a jingle, the AFM contract allows unlimited airplay and you receive only one fee every 13 weeks. It doesn't take a calculator to figure out who comes out ahead. Singers also make more money than their musician counterparts for records, theater gigs, industrial shows, theme songs – you name it.

In addition, when you add vocals to your arsenal, you instantly triple your employability. With your new skill, new opportunities will abound – from singing background vocals with a wedding band to doing the lead vocal on a film soundtrack. It doesn't hurt to take dancing lessons too; dancing improves your stage presence and builds your body confidence.

If I *still* haven't convinced you to start chirping, perhaps one of these thoughts will:

"Sing again, with your dear voice revealing
A tone
Of some world far from ours,
Where music and moonlight and feeling are one."
                            – *Percy Bysshe Shelley (1822)*

"Alas for those that never sing,
But die with all their music in them!"
                            – *Oliver Wendell Holmes (1858)*

"Yes, there will be singing in heaven, and when I get there I will want to have David with his harp, and Paul, and Peter and other saints gather around for a sing."
– *Peter Mackenzie (Wesleyan Preacher)*

"If you can walk you can dance. If you can talk you can sing."
– *Zimbabwean Proverb*

A Critique of Critics

One significant distraction for the modern musician is the over-whelming din of the media – specifically of entertainment "news" and music criticism. Though music critics help the average music fan sort through the plethora of CDs released each year, you should listen to and read the music press with a grain of salt; ignore reviews of your own work, particularly if they are favorable. (Do save them for your promo packages.)

We obviously need music critics, and they sure as heck need us. Unfortunately, many of them miss the mark badly, or are simply not qualified to cover more than one genre or era of music. Many of them do not write well. I'd also suggest that among all fields of criticism in the arts and humanities, music criticism is the most problematic: music is probably the most abstract art; it is more difficult to *listen* objectively than to *see* objectively; sound is much more flexible than the written word. Violinist Matt Glaser got it right when he said, "Music expresses things that cannot be expressed in any other way. When you attempt to find language to describe that, the words fall short." When one small-minded critic called Stravinsky's *Rite of Spring* "noise," the composer fired off a letter which declared that "talking about music is like dancing about architecture." [This last quote is commonly and erroneously attributed to either Laurie Andersen or Elvis Costello.] And remember: what the poets cannot express in words, the painters paint; what the painters cannot express in their paintings, the musicians play. Music speaks for itself.

Another annoying thing about many music critics is their penchant for lazy or inaccurate labels. Does "Jazz" mean Kenny G., Squirrel Nut Zippers, or Cecil Taylor? Can one critic write accurately and fairly about all of these artists? Conversely, do we need a hyper-specific, syntax-defying, mumbo-jumbo category name like "retro trip-hop industrial house trance"? Of course, this syndrome is not unique to the music business. A 1998 trial run of the U.S. census gave citizens the option to identify themselves as "White + Black + Asian + American Indian or Alaska Native + Native Hawaiian or Pacific Islander + Some Other Race." Yes, they were trying to identify one person. I do like one category name that I found on the Web: "Stuff That You Won't Find On The Radio."

The worst critics often create a labyrinth of hyperbolic circumlocution to describe nothing. Here is an example of such prose in *Rolling Stone*: "The energetic young things celebrate you-go-girl confidence and the dance-floor charms of suburban R&B with a sense of entitlement that is almost breathtaking – if they strut into their debut album like divas, well, they are divas ... [It] could pass for a boy-band album if the sexes were reversed – but this act is very clean. Sounds good, and, if you're under eighteen, good for you, too." So this is a music review? Oy.

The space these reviews occupy would be better used for introducing readers to new artists, and to artists without corporate sponsorship. Of course, we can't expect much when substance, content, and long-term career development are endangered species. Let the E! Channel tell tales of Fergie and Lady Gaga and perpetuate the same controversy-hungry publicity machine that handled Britney Spears. These artists are far less titillating or legitimately "subversive" than Elvis Presley, Janis Joplin, Bob Marley, Jimi Hendrix, Frank Zappa, David Bowie, Johnny Rotten, Prince, or The Rolling Stones in their heyday, and this "old" music is still very much with us. Jennifer Lopez's and Janet Jackson's infamous dresses and similar examples of fashion fun (or bubble gum exhibitionism) are scandalous and newsworthy? Does anybody remember Josephine Baker, Mae West, the Vargas Girls or Fritz the Cat? What about the can-can, go-go dancing and most of what's on television? We lost our innocence a long time ago, but don't tell that to the popular music press: they're in a tizzy over this great new gizmo called the "wheel."

Whether it's Ed Sullivan banning Elvis's pelvis, or the *New York Times* reprinting Eminem's lyrics for the umpteenth time and dismissing them as "inane and obscene," the net results are the same: the choir has been preached to, the machine has been oiled, and more ringtones are sold. It's enough to make you think about conspiracy theories or at least conflicts of interest: do all the critics secretly work for Disney? Regardless, it's the vast legions of wonderful but non-controversial musicians and unflashy bands that get lost in the PR shuffle.

Not everyone is duped by the smoke and mirrors. A levelheaded letter to the *Times* pointed out that Eminem is "just another performer, just another career." When all is said and done, it's the increasing power of the ignoble and greedy popular press, and the sorry state of the American educational system that should concern parents and other besieged citizens, and not the ebb and flow of art in the free world.

Regarding the myopic tendencies of some jazz and "serious music" critics, bassist and composer Darren Solomon puts it well: "[They] stake out a specific place on the musical evolution time line and wonder why the rest of the world is not standing still with them." It's understandable: to anyone with limited or closed ears, all music employing computers and samples sounds identical. These close-minded pundits don't acknowledge the fact that technology – be it in the form of a saxophone, an electric guitar or a synthesizer – has been intertwined with music for a long time; crappy music was invented long before computers. If I read one more review that lumps all "new" musical styles together, I'll have to write a letter.

To be fair, there are music critics who get it right, usually because they pick a musical niche, and spend a great deal of time listening to the music, researching its origins, and talking with the musicians who create it. They write as excellent musicians play: with command, dedication, passion, humor, imagination, and equal measures of accurate historical perspective and insightful, objective analysis. I think music critics are at their very best when they possess the necessary humility to focus on the *music*. In *The New Republic* (January 22, 2001), Leon

Wieseltier points out that "My [musical] pleasure is not more valuable than your pleasure." Thank you.

In summary, it's natural to hope that your next CD or concert gets reviewed by a wise, fair, sensitive, and articulate journalist, but don't count on it. And avoid becoming a pseudo-critic yourself: make sure you try to *feel* the music before you try to analyze it.

PART 3:
SELLING YOURSELF

Ultimately, your music should speak for itself.
But the music business often demands much more
than mere musical ability.

Sell *What* Out?

The other day one of my colleagues quipped, "Selling out is when you show up at the gig for the prime rib." Another added, "The word 'sellout' isn't in my vocabulary." I think many of us feel the same way.

The word "sellout" is misused, overused, and rarely applicable in the music business, which is – like all businesses – a commercial endeavor. I suppose that you're a sellout if you *purposely* abandon the principles you hold dear just to make money. However, you're in the minority if you have the ability to dupe your audience into buying something that you don't believe in. The general public can be fooled only temporarily – they eventually uncover and reject most fakers. Right now you're probably thinking of all the successful performers you can't stand, and preparing your rebuttal. But I challenge you to name one successful artist who's not at least thoroughly committed to their "product."

This word "product" bothers many musicians. Maybe if you just play for your friends and family – and don't charge them – you can avoid being labeled "commercial." But the second you're paid to play, you're selling a product: *you*. And commerce knows no artistic boundaries: "esoteric" or "high" art can be just as commercial as the Top 10 – sometimes more so. It's all about the ballyhoo. Many musicians subsidize their less accessible music with music that's easier to sell. Is that selling out? I don't think so. Bach served under the patronage of royalty and the church; you have more numerous potential patrons, such as advertising agencies, Broadway producers, touring superstars, nonprofit corporations, and government sponsors such as the National Endowment for the Arts.

It's great if you can make a decent living as a musician. If you can manage to make a living composing and playing only the music you love, you're doubly blessed. Concentrate on making the best music you can possibly make. If you believe in your work, you will usually have an easier time selling it. Whether you're playing or selling, people appreciate your sincerity.

Mirror Mirror

Thanks a lot, Elvis. Ya' had to be so darn good lookin'.

Beauty in our commercial culture is redefined by the minute. And, of course, beauty is in the eye of the beholder; one person's good figure is another's anorexia. Stand aside from this hyperactive fashion frenzy. Find *your own* style. Accentuate your unique attributes and experiment with clothing until you're comfortable with at least one stage look. There's usually something simple that will help – the right hat or haircut, for instance. Think of Lyle Lovett: no one can mess with *that* hair! The kids who teased him in the second grade now have to pay to hear him sing.

Developing an effective visual image is an integral part of selling yourself. Define your visual style clearly and make it mesh with your music; don't wait for an entertainment conglomerate to do it for you. Know thyself. PR departments and the media have the power to promote anything they choose, but they often simply copy the *latest* big thing, creating a large stylistic vacuum. Your goal is to be the *next* big thing. Learn from Madonna (and Sarah Bernhardt a century before her): they were self-styled icons who morphed frequently without losing their enormous popularity.

Knowing what's "in" has never been easier; simply watch E! and the Fashion Channel, go to new movies, and buy a few magazines. It's all there. But the avatars of fashion come and go, and if you're imitating the current look, you're already out of style. It's much more constructive, and ultimately creative, to draw inspiration from deeper and more stimulating sources – history, science, nature, and cultural traditions. If you have low self-esteem, or just don't know where to begin, ask a trusted (and fashion-savvy) friend to make style suggestions and to help you shop. And never compare your physical qualities to those of other people. In the heavily overpopulated music business, weird or different is good. Go ahead and get wacky – or at least a bit wacky. Superior visual presentations are especially helpful to musicians who play esoteric music, and want to broaden their appeal. Bjork knows this well, and uses elaborate costumes, makeup and props to great effect. Even if your band employs a professional stylist, it helps to know something about fashion.

"But I'm just a viola player," you say. A new look can work wonders for you too. Sometimes you just get bored with the way you look; try to develop an alternative persona. Your playing might blossom with your new image. Composer and keyboard wiz Paul Jacobs sums it up: "Good hair covers a lot of mistakes. A good lawyer covers the rest of them."

Be On Time. This Means You.

Though some employers place more emphasis on punctuality than others, make no mistake: they *all* notice when you're late. Worse, their displeasure might not be apparent until next time, when the call goes to someone else. A reputation for consistent tardiness can have a devastating effect on your career. Of course you will encounter musicians who are so revered and seemingly omnipotent, that they show up at will and go unpunished for years. But even Charlie Parker had to pay for his chronic unreliability: many of his best musicians simply left his band.

There are many reasons, besides drug addiction and all-consuming genius, why you will occasionally be late for work – even if it hasn't happened yet. Family crises, health problems, and traffic are often to blame. The typical full-time musician juggles normal life requirements with late club gigs, early recording sessions, road work, sound checks, rehearsals, practice routines, learning and memorizing songs, instrument maintenance, instrument cartage, teaching schedules, business calls, self-promotion, composing, and more. We all know that when the phone doesn't ring for a week or two, it means that the next five job offers will be gigs that will start within an hour of each other; most musicians have trouble saying 'no,' creating further havoc in their schedules. In addition to leaving more than enough time to get to work, follow these rules:

1) Carry the home phone, cellphone, and e-mail numbers of at least ten people that can cover a gig for you with less than an hour's notice.

2) If you have a particularly busy day scheduled (or come down with the flu prior to a busy day), call a sub or two in advance and see whether they'll be available, just in case. And while you're at it, check on their health, their families, and their latest professional triumphs.

3) If you know you'll be even one minute late, call your employer. This will allow him to effectively delegate his extra time. If he wants to reschedule or cancel you, be flexible. I cannot overemphasize the importance of this courtesy call.

4) When you arrive late – whether you called or not – always apologize but don't draw unnecessary attention to your faux pas; your colleagues will likely do that for you. Certain employers – Broadway contractors, for instance – simply won't invite you back.

5) If you're *very* late (usually anything over 20 minutes, depending on the gig), offer to take less money. It's a gesture that is always appreciated and rarely acted upon. Hopefully.

6) Even if there were no other reasons to be on time, you should show up early just to get accustomed to your surroundings and co-workers before you play.

7) Since you've now learned to be on time, arm yourself with enough reading material, listening devices, and portable work that you'll look forward to your pre and post-job "down" time.

8) Be aware that people who say punctuality is unimportant tend to be consistently late. It will eventually catch up to them.

9) If you want a chair in that Big Band In The Sky, also help your colleagues arrive on time.

Jammin' 'Til the Break of Dawn

One of best things you can do to advance your career – regardless of its state – is to sit in with bands at every opportunity. The benefits are numerous: you build confidence, expand your contact base, broaden your musical versatility, and you command the attention of the audience (and hopefully that of the club manager). If you screw up, you'll learn what you need to practice. *Something* good happens every time you hit the stage. And you can never be too good, too "important" or too rich to jam.

If you don't have an "in" with one of the band members, it's a good idea to talk to the bandleader before the set begins. This gives him a chance to properly assess your credentials, and to pick a song that works for you and the band. When asking to sit in, don't hesitate to sell yourself by mentioning your career highlights; though Miles Davis claimed he could determine a musician's ability by the way he walked, most bandleaders are mortal. If your request is denied, retreat gracefully – don't beg.

Sometimes you can succeed with a more spontaneous approach: unpack your instrument and approach the stage while the band is performing a song you want to solo on. If you look halfway hip, and the arrangement is loose enough, they might be curious enough to invite you up to play.

I've scored a ton of work from jamming with bands around the world. Sometimes it was a simple exchange of phone numbers that led to a gig years later. Other times I was hired for session work the next day. You should sit in with bands whenever you get the opportunity; it's good for you.

Similarly, if you're a bandleader, it's a good idea to invite people to jam with you. One of my favorite "sit-ins" happened when I was on tour with Steve Winwood. After we did a show in Montreal, Steve and some of the band went for a beer at our hotel bar. A somewhat jaded house band was on stage, and they were unaware of our arrival. After a few tunes and a few beers, a couple of us asked the lead singer if we could play with his band. He reluctantly acquiesced, and we motioned to Steve. Winwood was more famous than ever because he was touring behind a mega hit album, and when he approached the stage, drumsticks and mouths hit the floor. After they comprehended that Steve wanted to perform with (and not goof on) them, we played a few Traffic songs, much to the delight of the small, thrilled bar crowd. I'm certain that *this* hotel band – having received shock therapy – never sounded better, and that the bandleader will always hope that another rock icon will ask to sit in.

Here's My Card

Business cards may seem quaint to kids who do *everything* on their smartphones, but they're still important. Treat business cards with reverence: you can never tell which one might hold the key to good gigs, financial rewards, or new friends. Ask for them even if you've "made it" or if the cardholder is not an ace – he may become one. Plus, it makes people feel good. Dutifully copy their content to your database. Jot down key phrases that will help you remember them years later, like "excellent boogie woogie; knows Frieda" or "slightly touched; punched piccolo player."

Follow up on any commitments you make to card givers such as telling them you will e-mail them a website address or send them a CD. Even if you don't have a specific reason to contact them, call within a few months and say hello. Many musicians network diligently in spurts, usually when they're unemployed. Instead, make it routine – during feast or famine – but avoid calling too often. Maybe they were just being polite when they gave you their card, and don't really want to hear from you.

Obviously your own card should reflect your personality and your true forte(s). Musicians have creative license in card content, so use it to stand out from the crowd. One of the most effective cards I've ever seen looked like a napkin with handwriting on it. One pal of mine had a card that read "Bon Vivant and Raconteur," terms which describe him to a tee, and never failed to produce a smile.

Don't always wait for people to ask for your card – maybe they just forgot. And if someone does ask for your card, ask for one of theirs without hesitation.

Welcome to Japan!

Promote or Perish

There are numerous books and websites dedicated to the art of promotion, so I'll just touch on a few key points. Developing potent promotional (promo) material is one of the most important things you can do to advance your career. Even if you have a manager, an agent, a record deal and a publicist, you should learn the basics of effective advertising so you can know if they're doing their job correctly, and make savvy suggestions. The ballyhoo starts with you. Obviously the longer you work, the more opportunities you'll have to expand and enhance your promo package, but it's never too early (or too late) to put one together.

Remember that there's a fine line between being a good salesperson and a being a huckster; you'll know if you've crossed that line if you exaggerate as much as the protagonist in *The Music Man*. Too many superb musicians damage their artistic credibility with their big mouths. Jelly Roll Morton, after recording the classic Red Hot Peppers sessions – widely considered to be his best work – spent most of the rest of his life, in the words of George Hoefer, "suing the world for recognition." In response to a radio program that paid tribute to W.C. Handy, Morton fired off a letter to *Down Beat* in which he wrote "I myself happened to be the creator of jazz in the year of 1902." But it's true that 99% of all the performers we are familiar with *were* sold to us, either by the artists themselves, by their managers, publicists and record companies, or by all concerned.

All the components in your package should be consistent with your music, your personality, and with each other. It's crucial to make a clear, concise statement with each ingredient. Make sure each item can stand on its own so that you can customize your sales-pitch to individual employers and clients. Although you can put together a decent publicity kit on your own – and do it on a shoe-string budget – it's better if you can get help from a professional photographer, graphic artist, and writer. Here are the basic items you will need:

1) A killer **website**, and a presence on MySpace, Facebook, LinkedIn, and Twitter – whichever fits your vibe. Put videos of your band or yourself on YouTube (if they're good!). These web tools might make many of the following items seem irrelevant, but you should cover all the bases.

2) Your **CD** or **MP3** file**.**

3) A **cover, folder, or box** that can contain any printed and recorded material. This is your opening statement, and you should make it a memorable one. It should look great and feel solid; nothing should be able to fall out of it; the design, paper, colors, and print quality should be first rate.

4) An original, striking, and long-lasting **logo** that will appear on almost everything you hand out.

5) Your **biography**. It should be meticulously written, accurate, thorough, lucid, and contain no superfluous information. It's a good idea to prepare both full and condensed versions; some employers will want to read your life story, some will not.

The **full bio** should be a chronological story that includes your birth date and birth place, a synopsis of your early influences and education, awards you've won, a description of how you got your first break, all the important gigs you've done, information about your past recordings and your current projects, a brief story about what influenced the songs on your latest CD, and what you hope to accomplish in the future.

The **condensed bio** should be tailored to fit whatever job you're trying to get: devote fewer words to the past and more to the present;

don't include information about your education and awards unless they're remarkable or relevant, e.g. a masters degree in composition from Julliard, or a Grammy for song of the year; don't include any unrecognizable names or places:"Then I played for five weeks with Tony Tuneworthy at the DWI Bar in Aberystwyth."

6) A one-page **fact sheet** including only your most notable career highlights, information about your new CD and video, your current gig schedule, and your contact information.

7) **Photographs**. They should be of the highest quality. Make sure you have a minimum of three up-to-date photos to use: an 8 x 10 head shot, a live performance shot, and an informal picture with an attractive background, with or without your instrument. Your decision of whether to use color or black & white should be based on the total look of your package. You can use multiple photos if you do a montage – just make sure they mesh well.

8) **Reviews and press clips**. It may be obvious, but only include favorable press; if you get a lukewarm review from an illustrious publication, edit it down to a sentence or two, and feature an enlarged version of the magazine or newspaper logo. Don't hesitate to use old press, but make sure to enclose some recent items as well.

9) A **DVD** including live performance and recording studio footage, interviews, and people reacting to your music. Your mini epic should be interspersed with diverse informal shots; they can be beautiful, humorous, or shocking, but they should compliment your music and hold the attention of your target audience.

10) A short, simple and friendly **cover letter**.

Another item you can include is a little **gift** with your logo on it. Here are some suggestions:

a) The ubiquitous t-shirt or baseball cap.
b) A CD opener.
c) Custom packaged candy; Altoids are a safe bet.

d) Golf balls or Frisbees.

e) Magnets and mugs.

f) If your band is called "Smack That Gerbil," include a ... well, you get the idea.

Use the same creativity and high standards for your promo package that you use for your music. The overall effect can be flashy, strange, sexy, zany or intellectually challenging – as long as it looks great and represents you well. Put your bread where it counts: the music and video production, the website, and the packaging. As I previously mentioned, you won't need to give all of your material to everybody; some employers or managers will only want your CD, and then they might check out your website – others will request additional material, e.g. a summary of your career goals. Stay prepared by keeping the entire package updated so you don't have to scramble when important opportunities arise.

You can never build too many bridges.

Out of Sight ...

Beyond jamming, exchanging cards, and distributing promotional material, remember a fourth way to get "out there": go to concerts and clubs to see your friends play. In addition to supporting them, you let them know that you're not too cool to hang out, and that you don't just show up when shekels are involved. Also, go to non-musician parties and let people know that you're a musician. Good conversations (and possibly work) won't be hard to come by. Of course musicians spend many long, solitary hours studying, practicing, listening to, writing and transcribing music. *Do not become a hermit.* Most effective means of improving your visibility require that you leave your abode to achieve them.

But if you can't stand smoky clubs, dislike talking on the phone, or are generally clumsy in social situations, shy, or reclusive by nature, the Internet was made for you. It's also the most cost-effective promotional tool currently available. There are many books and magazines you can buy to guide you through the tangled World Wide Web, but here are my suggestions for the average musician:

1) In case you're one of the three people who haven't done so, sign up for Facebook, MySpace, Twitter, LinkedIn, CDBaby, iTunes – anything you can that gets you and your music out there.

2) Get a website. Since music is a crowded field, feature something special and specific and do it in a catchy way: broadcast a club gig live; put new samples of your playing and writing on the site weekly; offer a free t-shirt or Frisbee to the first hundred people that buy your CD. Dozens of sites and services allow you to create your own site cheaply or for free, but if you can afford one, hire a website designer.

3) Listen to Web radio stations. You can hear some pretty wild stuff on Radio Zimbabwe at 4 am. Listen to samples of artists you're unfamiliar with.

4) Visit sites, read blogs, and join discussion groups on subjects ranging from bassoon technique to the music of Sun Ra. Be sure to visit university sites from around the world: they are rich sources for the more obscure stuff, and you may find a faculty member or a class that you dig. Check out "iTunes U" for musician interviews and profiles.

5) Take a music class online.

6) Trawl around for information on auditions, jam sessions, concert schedules, and songwriting contests.

7) Download songs and sounds.

8) If you have a high-speed Internet connection, and computer-based recording software, you can record tracks using musicians playing on the other side of the world, or play on their tracks yourself.

9) Research entertainment law. Download sample contracts and review landmark rulings.

10) Do your music-related shopping – or at least comparison shopping – on the Web. From vintage tubas on Craigslist and eBay to CD fire sales at failing dot-coms, to the latest recording equipment at on-line music stores, the Web is the best way to shop since the Sear's catalogue.

There are thousands of publications dedicated to this subject. If you're just getting started, check out *Music Online for Dummies* by David Kushner, and *The MP3 and Internet Audio Handbook: Your Guide to the Digital Music Revolution* by Bruce and Marty Fries.

Matchmaker, Matchmaker

Putting bands together, recommending musicians for jobs, and hiring musicians to play for shows and recording sessions (formally known as "contracting") are some of my favorite activities. It's extremely satisfying to introduce a drummer to a bass player and discover they not only play well together, but achieve a symbiosis that many marriages never realize. Good musicians communicate at a very high level; watching and hearing the trust, sensitivity, and camaraderie that can develop among musicians who have just met is truly something to behold and "behear." Plus, with the exceptions of brilliant musicianship and a winning personality, nothing makes you look better than introducing musicians who hit it off; the happy couples will remember you fondly. And official contracting jobs pay well.

How do you become a successful matchmaker? Hiring musicians is a somewhat imprecise science: what seems to be an obvious musical match can self-destruct for non-musical reasons; I've seen musicians reject each other before they've ever played a note. Even the wrong handshake or clothes can result in a long, uncomfortable night, as musicians are notoriously sensitive about such matters. Picky picky! Putting two musicians together is similar to setting up two of your friends on a blind date: you're fond of both people and you have a hunch that they might get along; you make a couple of calls. If things work out, you're a bridesmaid or a best man. If the date is a disaster, you either come up with a new prospect or claim immunity. As in all areas of the music business you must develop a thick skin, and be willing to fail repeatedly without giving up.

Some matches are no-brainers: you hire or recommend musicians who have a solid track record, who show up on time, and who you just *know* will sound good – if unremarkable – together. But if you get a chance to stretch a little, you should also attempt to promote less obvious liaisons just to see what happens: a smart, musical rock singer can add a new dimension to a big band; a seemingly quiet, shy trumpet player may experience a musical epiphany when he plays with an exuberant funk drummer. Invite a Brazilian percussionist to play with your wedding band; introduce an older classical flutist to a young folk band. Of course, some musical love affairs take longer to develop than others. It's fun to try when your career's not on the line.

If you're a performer with a steady gig, or a producer with access to a studio, you have the luxury of auditioning musicians to determine which combinations are viable. I suggest that even if you don't have a band or a gig you should organize jam sessions or rehearsals just to sharpen your matchmaking skills. Develop the confidence to invite all kinds of musicians, including those who play the same instrument as you, and share information with them freely. If you have friends who are playing a "loose" club gig, ask them if they will allow one of your colleagues to sit in with them. Also remember who introduced you to various musicians and try to return the favor. Don't be afraid to network, and don't worry that networking will somehow taint your artistic sensibilities.

They Love Me, They Love Me Not

An audience can be your best friend or your worst enemy. Unless you don't care what people think about your music (a rare ability), it's a good idea to stack the odds in your favor. Bring your family and friends to every gig! You have plenty to concentrate on when you perform, and you don't need restless audience members and negative vibes distracting you. Audiences are as different and as unpredictable as the individuals that comprise them (even if you have a loyal fan base), but there are a few things you can count on.

First, if your band is wrong for the venue, you're bound for trouble. If you attempt to play jazz at a traditional rock club, you'll probably be unceremoniously rejected. Ask your colleagues about their favorite clubs. Get a feel for the venue by visiting it on at least two different nights before you ever talk with its booking agent or manager; the crowd on Tuesday is likely to be very different from the Friday mob. When you arrive at any gig, first try to get a read on the club employees, on the bar patrons, on the people in line outside the concert hall – whoever is around. From then on, pay attention to the collective mood in the room. Whenever you do a gig, take note of what works in the first set and apply what you learn to subsequent sets.

There's a "getting to know you" period at the beginning of every gig. Be patient. You usually need to play a minimum of three songs – sometimes a whole set – and say a few words into the microphone before you can determine whether the audience is on your side or not. In addition to shaking off the dust of the day, people's ears need to adapt to the club's acoustics, to the sound system, and to your brand of music. Next, if you don't talk to the audience, they will usually ignore you. And if you talk to the audience too much, they will usually ignore you. At bare minimum, welcome them to the show, introduce some of the songs, pay homage to your band members and to the people who work at the club, and thank everyone for being there at the end of each set.

Then, assuming that your band is well rehearsed – and that your music is compelling, pleasing to the ear, or danceable – have a good time. Every audience wants to see a hard-working band that does their job well, and enjoys doing it. Joy and enthusiasm are infectious. Of course, if you're playing in a place where alcohol is served, the audience will probably have a good time without your help. A drinking audience goes one of two ways: raucous and supportive, or rowdy and hostile. There isn't much you can do about this, other than going with the flow. If they like you, they like you more. If they hate you, they hate you more. More important, not everyone is going to like you or your music with or without alcohol; you must be somewhat immune to your detractors, and ignore the vitriolic audience members altogether. Similarly, you should ignore the "laughers," especially if they're laughing *at* you, and when they cackle during soft, subtle or sad songs.

Also working aggressively against you is the fact that the modern audience has been weaned on television, computers, multimedia entertainment, and superior home sound and video systems; they've seen and heard it all before – or at least believe they have, and their attention spans are almost nonexistent. Many sound systems put you at a disadvantage from the start, and you should speak with the house engineer about bringing your own gear to enhance the existing system. Always bring your own amp, microphone and cable, (and any other helpful devices you can easily carry) just in case the gig site has insufficient, low-quality, or broken equipment – or play without amplification. And pay attention to your visual presentation: it's expected (see *You Call That Entertainment?* and *Mirror Mirror*).

Don't be disappointed about a low reading on the applause meter, as clapping has almost gone out of style; it's often vocal exhortations, or nothing at all. I'm always amazed when I play for crowds that bob and sway, shout and boogie in ecstasy and close their eyes in moments of apparent rapture – and then remain quiet at the end of a song. After the set, many of the same people come up to me and gush. Though this has always been the norm in New York, it's increasingly common elsewhere. Anyway, don't let the overwhelming silence suck the energy out of your performance – your new fans are out there, and they want to love you.

If you make your living playing in bars, accept the fact that you will have to deal with numskulls and alcoholics on a regular basis. (Unfortunately, more than a few of them are club owners, managers and bartenders.) Bars are breeding grounds for that lowlife saboteur, that self-important agitator, that penultimate punk – the heckler. It's worse when they come in packs, urging each other on to ever-greater heights of obnoxiousness. And it's still more challenging if you're female and have to deal with a humongous, dumb, sexually aggressive, plastered male. As I pointed out in *You Call That Entertainment?*, it helps to have the audience in your corner from the get-go. Try – with the help of the crowd – to make hecklers part of the show.

During a gig I played with Ben E. King at the Blue Note, a tourist in the front row started blathering and bellowing about race relations and shouting song requests. Since we were making a live recording, the stakes were particularly high. King, a smart showman, immediately came off the stage to give our troublemaker a private concert, singing sweetly about three inches from the guy's face, which completely overwhelmed him. When the song ended, King took two minutes to pay *homage* to his "best fan" and said, "Isn't it beautiful that this man has a memory like that? Let's hear it for him." He *smothered* the heckler with love. The rest of the audience – after first expressing hostility towards the tourist – was touched and humored. The man smiled and didn't make a peep for the rest of the set. You can't always count on a similar result; sometimes you have to give up and signal for help from the bartender, bouncer or manager. But try to make friends first.

When all is said and done, you're there first to make great music, second to entertain people, third to make a good living, and fourth to have a good time. Make no mistake about it though: it is the audience that creates the demand for your services and you owe your entire career to them. Show them your appreciation and respect – and they will probably return the favor.

To Sign or Not To Sign

(Or "Mr. Toad's Wild Ride")

Things ain't what they used to be.

Here I aim to give you a picture of how the current record business got where it is and to help you decide whether to even pursue a record deal. Since the business is constantly changing, you should stay up-to-date by reading *Billboard* and other trade papers as well as the business and arts sections in your newspaper, by talking with your colleagues, and by scanning the Web for music news.

It's easy to get discouraged by the current state of affairs: it seems as if *everyone* has recorded *something*; finding a toehold on such a crowded cliff is daunting. But you should make your own CD if only to learn how to do it, and to have *something* to hand out as opportunities arise. If you're a songwriter, you're already familiar with the drill: Wait until you have "something to say," and then wait for nothing or no one. Making my first CD was one of the most difficult but fulfilling and educational experiences I've ever had. Though I have yet to go platinum, my CD opened up numerous doors, spawned a few jingles and a TV theme, and set the stage for more efficient (and hopefully better-sounding) future efforts.

One way through this labyrinth is to sign a production deal: A producer, or a production team, believes in you enough to work on spec; he hires and pays for the studios, musicians, engineers, equipment, and any post-production costs; if you get signed, he will typically recoup his investment plus a fee, produce some or all of the tracks, and receive a percentage of the income generated by the record. Ideally, this producer is well-connected and has a clear idea of which company will sign you. In fact he may already work *for* a record company which will bankroll the project. Obviously it helps if you're already friendly with a producer or two, and have good material and a strong identity to back it up. As in any business, half the battle is being at the right place at the right time with the right product. The other half is knowing the right people.

Another route is to do it yourself. If you don't have abundant financial resources, it's a good idea to get an investor or a low-interest loan to help fund your recording project – even if you eventually want to sign with a major label; plentiful cash will fuel your efforts, give you more options, make life easier, and will probably help you create a superior product. To find cash, look to obvious sources first: If your family is unable or unwilling to help you, ask your wealthier friends and colleagues if they're interested; see if your bank, credit union, or musician's union offers low-cost loans. If the coffers are still empty, ask everybody – especially your fans, people in the finance industry, lawyers, recording studio heads and other business owners – if they know any "angels." When you find someone who's willing to help, make sure that you both sign a contract before any checks are written. Ideally, the agreement should include a generous return to your investor if the project succeeds, and a generous amount of time for you to repay the principal if your project is a commercial flop.

When you make a record, keep these four goals in mind:

1) Be true to yourself. Make music that *you* enjoy listening to.

2) Never underestimate spontaneity. Sometimes it's the wacky idea, the late night board mix, the accidental distortion on the snare, or the studio beagle baying in the background that makes a song come alive. If you can, record live in the studio or at a gig; simultaneously capture the moment and save money.

3) Maintain the highest possible standards for the recording (from tracking to mastering), the songs, the production, the performances, and the design.

4) Your CD is a document of you or your band's creative abilities *at the time you record it*. You can re-record and re-mix *forever* without actually improving the music. In fact, excessive tinkering can ruin a recording. (Of course, some artists ignore all reasonable time and budget constraints and become Steely Dan.) After you finish the basic tracks, step away to give your ears a rest. When you listen to your music again, you will know where you stand. Any changes or additions you need to make will be obvious and probably justified. Repeat this process one more time before you mix. Then, stop spending money and slap a bar code on that puppy!

Following is an overview of the recent history and the current state of the record business to help you make an informed choice regarding whether or not to sign on the dotted line:

The story of the music business in the 20th and early 21st centuries is one of tumultuous change – a perpetual Wild Wild West. It is characterized by dramatic business and personal wars between multinational corporations, private equity firms, pop superstars, producers, composers, sheet music publishers, record companies, phonograph and sound equipment manufacturers, radio and television broadcasters, websites, record pirates, ASCAP, BMI, SESAC, AFM, SAG, AFTRA, the Office of Copyrights, Congress, the President, and organized crime. It is fueled by astronomical sums of cash and an overstocked pool of talent. These forces defined and redefined the destinies of musicians, adding potholes to an already rough road. Fortunately, the power of great music helps us to survive this unholy chaos, and keeps us creating despite all odds. The music business is even *enjoyable* at times, but deciding how much of it to embrace is a complex choice.

The fortunes of independent (indie) record companies have been particularly volatile, partly because the majors have appropriated every indie innovation. The indies achieved spectacular success throughout the 1940s with "race" and "hillbilly" music, and ignored two long AFM recording bans that devastated the major labels. The majors responded by starting subsidiary labels with "sepia," "ebony" or "hick" departments, and developed well-funded "relationships" with disk jockeys. Big radio stations essentially functioned as advertising arms for the big labels.

The 1970s saw unprecedented increases in record sales. It was also a time of lavish excess which cut into profits and led to a mini-depression and subsequent restructuring at the end of the decade. The chasm between the winners and the losers widened as a handful of superstars negotiated enormous advances for their records. Large record companies supported their artists, paid for the production and promotion of the product, and recouped their expenses from record sales, licensing agreements, and most (or all) of the publishing revenue. Even if a record made a large profit – a rare event, especially in the days when cocaine for the engineer was part of the budget – most "blue collar" artists didn't see much money after they received their (less generous) advances, which were also recouped from future royalties. They made their living from touring (still the case), or from songs they wrote that got extensive radio play, or from mechanical royalties – royalties generated by each record sale paid to writers and publishers – for the infrequent hit record.

In the 1980s the majors went on a shopping spree buying up every indie they could find; signing a deal with a major record label became the *only* viable way to get your music to the public. Record companies increasingly put their marketing muscle behind a limited number of mega-selling superstars; those lucky race horses essentially financed the rest of the company's artist stable. The industry embraced MTV, recognizing it as a powerful advertising tool, and unknowns like Duran Duran rocketed to the top of the charts overnight courtesy of expensive videos, the cost of which were (again) recoupable from artist royalties. The possibilities of scoring a hit, gaining tour support, and being the focus of ego-boosting promotional campaigns kept musicians signing wildly exploitive contracts through the end of the 20th century.

Records made by established stars have always had the best chance of making a profit, but opposing forces have always been at work. In 1979 The Police bucked the "bigger is better" trend when they self-financed their record *Outlandos d'Amour, gave* the finished product to A & M Records, took little or no advance, but negotiated an unusually high royalty rate. The company had nothing to lose, and was able to put the entire budget into promotion. A song from the album ("Roxanne") was a smash hit, and the rest is history. Though this type of contract existed prior to the Police, the success of "Roxanne" had a profound influence on the way record deals were structured thereafter, and reminded everyone in the business that making a great and popular record didn't have to break the bank – something that jazz producers had known for years (think "Take the 'A' Train" or "The Girl From Impanema").

Other performers helped to dismantle the status quo of the 80s. The Grateful Dead urged their fans to record the band's live performances, borrowed or bought the masters, and built a lucrative mail order business around packaging and selling those same recordings back to their fans. The band also encouraged their fans to sell bootleg copies of their records, believing that this would help them build a bigger, more devoted fan base than most bands could dream of; they were right – and prophetic. Singer/songwriter Ani DiFranco also bypassed the big labels, selling millions of records on her own label beginning with her debut, *Ani DiFranco* (Righteous Babe, 1990). After years of traditional record contracts and relative obscurity as a solo artist, Aimee Mann was nominated for a Grammy for her first indie CD. According to Nielson SoundScan, by the industry peak in the summer of 2000, indies accounted for 16.3% of all retail record sales in the United States.

Had indies arrived again? Well, only if you believe in smoke and mirrors.

Enter the Internet – which has forever changed the way music is promoted and distributed. At first, transferring audio files over the Internet was a cumbersome, time-consuming process. Highly compressed, mono and "dirty" sounding recordings – interrupted by slow transfer times – were the norm. Also, the Internet was still considered to be some kind of new democracy, exempt from the normal rules of capitalism. As the technology improved, you could listen to good quality stereo music on the Web, or – here was a sea-change – download it for your own use. Predictably, many Web-entrepreneurs, record pirates, and just about everyone else saw this as a gift from Above – finally, an easy way to usurp copyright laws, ignore the all-powerful media conglomerates, and make a ton of money. And it worked – at least until the record companies, along with the RIAA, successfully sued and forced MP3.com to pay royalties, and sought to annihilate Napster and other "free" music sites.

The giant corporations arrived late to the Web music party and were under siege as a consequence. In response, they tried to buy, sue or forge profitable deals with *all* their rivals. But their business model had been turned upside-down (again): having experienced free music on the Web, the public expected more of the same – plus cheap films, books, games and other entertainment products that compete directly for the leisure dollar. At first, CD sales were flat or up: consumers who listened to or downloaded music from the Internet tended to purchase more CDs. But by 2001, CD sales were off – way off – and retail record stores began a fast death march. Though part of this decline was due to a worldwide economic slump, Napster and newer music swapping services such as Audio City, Grokster, Kazaa and Morpheus also played a significant role. In 2003, iTunes blew the model to smithereens by selling high quality, low-priced, *legal* downloads. Though stores like Walmart, Target and Starbucks temporarily picked up the slack in physical CD sales, the current recession has all but eliminated that trend too.

Since 2000, total album sales have declined by about half, even though digital music purchases are rising. In 2008, for example, physical album sales fell 20% to 362.6 million from 450.5 million in the previous year, while digital album sales rose 32% to a record 65.8 million according to Nielson SoundScan. This trend continued in 2009, but with less intensity: sales of individual digital tracks increased by 27% in 2008 and only by 8.3% in 2009. Ironically, as digital downloads reached a milestone, vinyl album sales also climbed. In 2009, 2.5 million vinyl albums were purchased, more than any other year since Nielsen SoundScan began tracking sales in 1991. Also – here's a little surprise – *illegal* downloads have leveled off, mainly because of the generally superior quality of legal downloads. And in 2009, Taylor Swift, a talented teenage singer/songwriter with an internet presence, had the best-selling album of the year, *Fearless* – narrowly beating Susan Boyle and Michael Jackson. Her label, Big Machine, is an indie.

Today, many record contracts are conceived and executed by an unholy mix of lawyers and more lawyers, production teams with an eye on their short-term profit margins, and A&R (artist and repertoire) divisions with an allegiance to everything but the artists and repertoire. Four conglomerates (Universal Music Group, Sony Music Entertainment, Warner Music Group, and EMI Group) swallowed up most of the large indies in the 1980s and 90s, and run what's left of the show. "Downsizing" and "Outsourcing" are the goals of the day: in order to cut costs, the majors created indie "shells" to use as subcontractors, and fully or partially purchased the independent distribution companies. Taylor Swift's record, for example, is distributed by Universal.

Like subcontractors in other industries, most music subcontractors use non-union labor and ignore collective bargaining agreements. The concentration of power among a small number of corporations at the top, combined with dispersed production and distribution among many small indies have significantly eroded the bargaining power of professional musicians and the AFM. Legitimately independent record labels no longer represent a challenge or an alternative to corporate control of the entertainment industry.

Conflicts of interest abound, and precious little emphasis is placed on long-term artist development. Many musicians sign record contracts early in their careers that give them little leverage in the future. Many are dropped after one record. Record companies have the right to keep artists under contract for many years, or sue them if they don't deliver a specified number of recordings. This practice is particularly frustrating to musicians who "outgrow" their labels or change their musical direction. Also, the rank-and-file musician wins only when tour budgets and musical styles sustain demand for their services, or when they have enough clout to command large fees. These factors have driven most musicians to reassess their options and seize their own destinies.

The Internet has created plentiful opportunities for determined independent artists, bands and tiny labels that no longer have to distribute their music via legions of middlemen. It's a simple and relatively inexpensive technical process to make a CD, and sell it over the Internet by signing up with a service that handles both physical and digital sales, such as CDBaby.com. Or, you can put some of your music on the Web for strictly promotional purposes, and – if your fan base increases – make good lunch money by selling bushels of CDs at your well-attended gigs. The Web has also opened some ears: consumers who shop on the Web can hear snippets of all kinds of music as they browse – one of the best things about this technology. If you're playing esoteric or complex music that never sold well in the first place, you're a winner!

Clearly, changes are afoot, and you have a few decisions to make: Do you have relationships with people in the record business? Are you willing to enter Lawyerville and play musical chairs with a damaged giant? Do you make the type of music that they are willing and able to market effectively? Or do you have the energy, resources, and persistence to go it alone? Who will produce your record? Do you love your own music enough to spend long, often frustrating hours trying to sell it? Either way, you will see many more changes in technology, marketing, public demand, and in the types of entertainment available. There's nothing like a cataclysm to liven things up.

Don't let these changes and obstacles daunt you. Pick a poison. Record!

See you in the Top 10.

I recommend that you read five incisive, meticulously researched books which thoroughly examine entertainment law, publishing and spec deals, record contracts, and much more: *This Business of Music* and *More About This Business of Music* by Sidney Shemel and M. William Krasilovsky, *All You Need To Know About the Music Business* by Donald S. Passman, *Studio Stories* by David Simons, and *American Popular Music Business in the 20th Century* by Russell Sanjek and David Sanjek. Be advised that the latter book is unusually "fact packed." Also, as usual, you can find plenty of useful information on the Web.

The Pits

Drummer and Broadway house contractor Warren Odze has been around – and down (in the pits, that is). Over the years, he's played with Judy Collins, Peter Allen, Astrud Gilberto, Hank Jones, Johnny Hartman and many others. He's also done a ton of Broadway shows, including *Shrek the Musical, Lennon, Thoroughly Modern Millie* and *The Wedding Singer*. If you are lucky enough to meet or play with him, you'll probably feel like you've known him your whole life.

DW: What's the first record you listened to more than once?

WO: The Chipmunks.

DW: Same here! Excellent marketing ... Why did you choose the drums?

WO: My neighbor across the street had a snare drum and I was infatu- ated with it.

DW: Who are some of the musicians and teachers who influenced you most?

WO: My drum teacher when I was young, Al Pollick. Later on, Buster Balley, Walter Rosenberger, Jo Jones, Elvin Jones, Beatles, Steve Gadd and Frank Sinatra to name a few. Everyone you play music with is an influence. They either have something desirable in their playing that you want to emulate and integrate or ignore.

DW: What was your first paid gig, and how did you get it?

WO: Hard to remember that long ago, but I was in a band and we played dances so I could have been twelve or thirteen.

DW: What's your current gig?

WO: I'm the drummer for *Come Fly Away* on Broadway.

DW: The Broadway pit is a mystery to most people. Please enlighten us.

WO: I would first ask them if they understood what playing on Broadway really means. Lots of people want to make the money but might be in denial about the real task. The ability to play at a concert level, give 150% eight times a week, and play the same music in the same venue might not be for everyone. It's like a recording session where you never get a take, but keep trying over and over again.

   Also, it's important to let subs come in and play so they don't get rusty. Part of the privilege of having the chair of a show is keeping the subs well oiled. And you should get out and play other music or just take a day off and do something unrelated.

DW: If someone out there *still* wants to try to break into that scene, how do they go about it?

WO: For Broadway and every other gig, we are our own best promoters and agents; how we conduct ourselves and play is the best advertising we have. It's also very important to play all kinds of music in all kinds of situations. Like a film score, a Broadway show travels through multiple musical styles. If a show includes some big band music, it's going to be hard to sound convincing unless you've played in a big band. Do you just do tune ups, or can you fix a car?

Also, there are more opportunities to get started by subbing in off-Broadway pits. The pay is not as good as Broadway so the need for subs is greater. These are the same musical directors and orchestrators who work on Broadway; it's a great chance to meet people and let them see what you can do. And the days of a music contractor putting together a full band are gone. The composer, orchestrator, conductor – even the choreographer – have a say. One more thing: a positive attitude is everything.

DW: Lately the music business has resembled a Greek Tragedy. Where do we go from here?

WO: Well, we have been automated haven't we? Things keep changing and you must live in the times you're in. That means different things to different people. I'm always amazed when I talk to musicians today about all the different things they do to piece together a living. I would hesitate to tell someone to become a professional musician in today's world unless they were prepared to be the best; there's no room for mediocrity. There will always be musicians and always be music, but the day-to-day kind of jobs that existed in the past – like studio work – are greatly reduced.

But if someone has a burning desire to express themselves through music, there's no stopping them. Most people that I know professionally were like that as kids. Passionate. The people with that desire and a great disposition will thrive; they always have and always will.

And there has never been a more important time to be in the arts than now. The arts are the education of the soul, and these are not very soulful times. The arts help us to feel and grow. It's my suspicion that people are starved to feel things these days, given how high-tech and fast the world moves.

DW: While we're at it, what is the meaning of life?

WO: James Taylor says "enjoying the passage of time." It might be that simple. We all come out of the gate with different pluses and minuses, and whatever cards got dealt, we have to work through it all with some kind of joy. Friends, spouses, children. I don't think anyone on their death bed said: "If I only did that one more gig."

DW: Thank you Warren.

PART 4:
PHILOSOPHICAL AND SPIRITUAL GUIDANCE

A few thoughts on how various aspects of life affect your music. Questions to ponder regarding your career.

Great Expectations

We all know that hard work and brilliant musicianship do not guarantee financial success, or any acknowledgment at all. History is littered with brilliant, neglected and destitute musicians of every persuasion. It makes sense, then, to approach music and the music business with low expectations and high aspirations; set lofty goals but avoid assigning a specific value to them (unless you're as great as Cole Porter who said, "My sole inspiration is a telephone call from a producer"). Conversely, don't sell yourself short. Your labor is worth something, and you should not hesitate to ask to be paid for it. Just be prepared for a skewed ask/receive ratio.

I'm proud to say that I share my astrological sign with both Louis Armstrong and the Queen Mother. Supposedly, part of the royal Leonine MO is acute laziness, modified by occasional bursts of powerful, lion-like energy. I'm afraid that this describes me well. As a musician, I have to fight this tendency with dogged determination; if I did not, I would never practice, never sit in, never accept challenging gigs, and definitely never write this book. In this business you are usually your own boss; only *you* can make yourself get up in the morning and practice arpeggios.

But maybe you were born under a different sign. I know a lot of cats and kittens that are so success-driven that you can hear it in their music. And it sounds awful. They live their lives in a terminal state of disappointment: "How come I'm not a star yet? I look better, dance better, and sound better than everyone in Peoria. What gives?" Chill, Simba. If dreams of stardom are your sole catalyst, get in line. Those art-as-sport people who *do* win often pepper the airwaves with the worst sonic dreck.

The most practical goal to cherish is balance. Learn and play music for music's sake. Approach the business with patience and perseverance. Be thankful when your hard work *is* rewarded, and protect your assets once you have them. Keep in mind that failure is often the first step on the ladder of success (think of the Beatles, who were turned down repeatedly until George Martin came along). Work on your goals one step at a time, and give yourself enough time to accomplish them. Raise the bar, and jump higher, but know when to rest. Don't apply the same pressure to other people that you apply to yourself.

And, finally, buy sensible books like this one.

No Respect

"**W**hen ya' gonna get a *real* job?"

Even the most well-intentioned family member is capable of asking such a nasty question. I was lucky: my family believed in and supported my music habit. Unfortunately, many of my colleagues have experienced just the opposite. Even after they achieved some measure of success, their career choice was frowned on by those people near and dear to them. And the musicians who have yet to "make it" or never do? At minimum, they get more than their share of "I told you so's." Perhaps more insulting is when someone sees you with an instrument or hears you play and asks, "So what do you do for a living?" This image of the beleaguered, unemployed musician has some truth in it. As I mentioned above, our business is one in which the supply far outweighs the demand.

But our plight is also a result of how little our country values its artists: among rich democracies, the United States ranks last in funding for the arts; what little we have is gradually going down the tubes, and there's no Medici family to save us. Corporate and private funding for the arts, though substantial, is skewed towards large and already successful organizations and rarely benefits the rank-and-file musician. In 2008, with the economy in shambles, that funding evaporated and one orchestra after another folded. What can we expect in a country that accents "free-market" solutions to community problems and strongly discourages the assertion of broader public interests? Ironically, when American artists perform abroad, they are often treated like royalty.

In addition, musicians *are* outside the norm: many of us dropped out of school; our hours are erratic; our dress code is extremely flexible (perpetual Casual Fridays); we have a somewhat out-of-date reputation for drug abuse and sexual promiscuity; when many "normal" people are thinking "house/kids/car," many of us are thinking "hotel/groupies/bus." Our behavior – and our past – makes us easy targets for the morals police who have successfully eroded government funding for the arts.

To make matters worse, the public is ignorant of who we are. Most people have no concept of the amount of time, talent, energy, discipline, and perseverance that it takes to be a good – let alone financially successful – musician. Most of us stay the course because we love it. Yet some misguided folks treat musicians with contempt – even more humiliating than pity.

But there's another side to this coin.

You also hear people say, "It must be *so* satisfying to make a living doing something you love" and "You're so lucky that you don't have to show up at the office every morning." And, of course, everyone wants to be a rock-and-roll star. Almost fifty years after the Fab Four hijacked our psyche, our kids are playing the *The Beatles: Rock Band* video game, and the Fab Faux fills auditoriums; the *Mama Mia!* franchise has grossed more than $2 billion in the last ten years; "American Idol," MTV, VHl, and CMT are going strong; TV shows, films and video games that feature musicians abound; devoted fans flock to clubs and concerts; pop stars dominate the fashion biz; music downloads inundate the Internet servers. TV, film and commercial composers – not to mention our pop, country, rap, opera and rock stars – are some of the richest people on the planet. Major orchestras, Broadway and TV shows, touring superstars, record producers and jingle houses provide ample employment for many musicians, despite the recent recession. We had a saxophone-tooting president, and one of our most famous cartoon icons, Lisa Simpson, plays the blues on her baritone sax. Even former Fed Chairman Alan Greenspan was a saxophone player: he played in a big band alongside bebop great Al Cohn. Maybe it's hip to be a musician after all.

It boils down to the haves and the have-nots: you're successful in America only if you're *commercially* successful; money buys respect. But do we really care? We have our craft and each other. All we can do is continue to make great music, and gently educate our fellow citizens about our profession, and show them how dedicated we are. Then we must hope that they shower us with the love and respect that we deserve. If we become rich in the process, let's hope we can maintain our perspective and sound good to boot.

Every Man is an Island

Perhaps Mark Twain was writing about the music business when he wryly observed: "Few of us can stand prosperity. Another man's, I mean." Stay focused on your own Muse. If you do, you'll have no time to compare your artistic or financial success to that of others.

Almost everybody experiences some degree of envy, if not outright jealousy. Some people wallow in this destructive emotion. People are likely to feel especially deprived when they live in places or work in industries where the gap between rich and poor is the widest; there's no business like show business to bring out covetous feelings in the best of us. In cultural paradises like New York, London, Paris, and San Francisco, the competition is particularly stiff. There are usually at least fifty people that do something similar to what you do – only better – and get paid more than you to do it. Even if you're a leader in your chosen field, it's only a matter of time before a younger, brighter, faster, and better looking replacement comes to town. Word spreads quickly through the musician grapevine about who got the latest tour, record deal, or TV show, and who "sounded incredible" on their last gig. Conversely, there are legions of less "gifted" musicians getting paid beaucoup bucks while their more talented colleagues languish.

Ignore it all. You will lose your mind if you pay attention to this trivial stuff. In a world where a seventeen-year-old pop singer of dubious talent buys a 27 million dollar house in Beverly Hills while the typical jazz musician struggles to pay her rent on time, you need to keep your eye on the prize. Just the fact that you are less hungry, and more prosperous, healthy and free than 90% of the world's population should make you feel extremely lucky. Moreover, people with seemingly insurmountable problems, such as Harriet Tubman, Hellen Keller, Chick Webb and Stephen Hawking, made remarkable contributions to mankind – partly because they focused on the work at hand; the word "self-pity" was not in their vocabularies.

The root of jealousy is insecurity, and most musicians are terribly insecure despite their frequent displays of bravado. If you're a serious musician, you don't have time to compare your music – let alone your bank account – with anyone. If you can't avoid being a tad jealous here and there, let this unholy feeling motivate you to practice more. James Taylor gives us another simple blueprint for success:"Keep your overhead down; avoid a major drug habit; play every day, and take it in front of other people. They need to hear it, and you need them to hear it." Anything else is unnecessary baggage.

Scuttlebutt, Poppycock, and Mumbo Jumbo

"We are cruel enough without meaning to be."

– John Updike in *Rabbit Is Rich* (1981)

In the dog-eat-dog world of the music business, it's easy to forget the inherent good in one's fellow man. That some of your colleagues have pronounced evil streaks is not in question. But when even the most well-intentioned musicians congregate to chew the fat, the line between "friendly gossip" and slander is often extremely thin. Rumors fly and before you know it, some poor tuba player has a tarnished reputation. Fair and intelligent debates over someone's musical strengths and weaknesses are one thing; speculation on and analysis of their personal lives is something else. Musicians who spread whoppers regarding other musicians should be punished by having to spend the rest of their careers schlepping equipment for a bad wedding band.

Sometimes gossip is the spawn of jealousy; musicians spread falsehoods with the intention of taking down a rival and try to boost their own egos by celebrating other people's misery. Other times, rumors rise from the ashes of a simple misunderstanding. But more often, the gabfest ringleader is a blabbermouth who specializes in hearsay, or just a loquacious schmuck. Don't touch this fungus – it can eat you alive. Don't stoop to the level of our muck-slinging politicians. Go to the source; check the facts. Or, more simply, mind your own business.

The speculation and chicanery ranges from the not-so-subtle dig ("He's got a gambling problem"), to the double slam ("She never returns calls and she's fat"). The advanced hornswaggler plays one *jazz* gig with his future victim, and goes around telling everyone that "he can't play *rock*" or "he's too expensive."

Then there are the *professional* rumor mills. Though I have yet to be written up in the *National Enquirer*, I've been the target of enough malarkey-mongering to sympathize with the tabloid victims whose only mistake was becoming famous. Par for the course you say? Comes with the territory? Probably so. But don't join the falsehood flingers, because it will come back to bite you. And if someone is spreading lies or embellished stories about you, your best defense is to do nothing, as the perpetrator will eventually slip up or earn his own bad rep and come crashing down to earth. Hopefully he won't land on top of a good Samaritan like you.

As some great sage once said, "Shut up 'n' play yer guitar."

A Note on the Big Picture

You are here to make great music. Let historians, sociologists and music critics quarrel about their personal preferences, artistic standards, and the historical and social contexts of music. It's difficult enough to learn how to play and write music, sustain a career in the music business, and live your life without having to analyze whether every song you play is politically correct, or how your music will be remembered. Many protest songs are written by people who could stand to learn more about both music *and* politics. It certainly doesn't hurt to try your hand at this art; the world needs all the positive vibes you can muster. Just don't make "message" music your sole mission unless you *know* you have a calling.

You can do little to combat *prejudice*, which is only one of the many faces of ignorance. However, as both a citizen and as a musician you do have to deal with the hydra of sex, race, and age *discrimination*. The music business is a stomping ground for this monster. Until very recently, female musicians – no matter how talented – were not welcome in the testosterone-filled club and studio fraternities, even when the singer or songwriter was female. In 1901, the AFM showed its true colors by trying to ban ragtime and all other manifestations of "The Negro School." Even today women and minorities are systematically excluded from the plum jobs at record companies. While all serious jazz musicians pay homage to white composers like Jerome Kern, Vernon Duke, Richard Rodgers, Harold Arlen, Irving Berlin, Cole Porter and George Gershwin, as well as white performers like Bunny Berigan, Benny Goodman, Frank Sinatra, Artie Shaw, Paul Desmond, Stan Getz and Bill Evans, many jazz critics and some jazz musicians attempt to portray jazz as an exclusively African American art form. Many rap and country impresarios don't practice equal opportunity employment. And, of course, the music industry is brutal for anyone over 29: age-related "attrition" is rampant in our business; most performers in the Top-Forty are barely out of high school. In summary, all chauvinists were created equal.

Though you probably won't be the hero that slays the monster, there are a few things you can do. First, be great: there's no revenge like artistic success. Second, be bold: report labor law violations to the proper authorities. Then, set a good example: don't hire or work for bigots; reject discrimination; treat your employees well; support the arts, your union, and other worthy causes; play at benefits, churches and hospitals in poor neighborhoods; educate your children; vote. In other words, walk the walk.

And never lose the faith that music heals the spirit, transcends hatred, and brings people together; if you're "only" an accomplished musician, composer or entertainer, you are already contributing to the benefit of mankind. But remember that there are only two types of musicians (and people) in the world: good and bad (though they come in every size, sex, age, color, religion, and yes, political affiliation). Hire, work for, and be the former. *Then* write some protest songs.

Excess and Debauchery

So many drugs, so little time. And they're free! No wonder everyone wants to be a rock and roll star. Eubie Blake summed it up:

"If I'd known I was going to live this long, I'd have taken better care of myself."

If you're strung out, you're probably not reading this book. Or you're already dead. If you're the typical binge drinker, you don't need anyone to tell you how you feel – excess is its own punishment. If your life resembles that of Micky Rourke's character in *Barfly*, clean up your act.

I've known many performers who could probably use *something* to loosen them up before they play, and others who sound terrible when they drink one beer and would benefit by quitting altogether. One thing is clear: when you drink or use drugs, your sense of pitch changes. I'll never forget when I first heard a tape of myself performing after a few too many; I sure *thought* I was playing in tune during the gig ...

Several of my colleagues are recovering alcoholics or former blow/smack/potheads who – though they're still brilliant musicians – all say that drugs ruined some of their musical abilities and various aspects of their lives. Some of them forget melodies in the middle of a performance. Some of them quickly tire. Others destroyed relationships with loved ones, or lost their apartment or their driver's license.

While you're at it, stop smoking too. If you play a wind instrument or sing, smoking anything will compromise your breathing and your ability to sustain a note, and eventually kill you.

If you think you *need* drugs or alcohol to perform well in any area of your life – especially music – take a hard look at yourself; listen when your employers, friends and family tell you that they're worried about you; don't be too proud to admit you have a problem or too embarrassed to seek help.

The Swami Told You to do *What*?

I grew up in that mecca of the counter-culture, Berkeley, California. There were so many alternative lifestyles available that many people forgot from what they were escaping. By the time I was five, I had learned more about transcendental meditation than baseball; later I dabbled in yoga, organized religion, exotic diets, astrology, and other life aids. I've also spent a great deal of time discussing these subjects with my colleagues.

Musicians as a breed are enthusiastic about anything that can help them relieve the stress of their relatively erratic lifestyles, and unleash their creative energy. Consequently, they're vulnerable to fads, fanatics, and fetishes. Though there are many worthy alternative lifestyles to try, don't let tai chi and chai tea rule your life. Don't practice Feng Shui more than you practice the piano.

You might find that something helps your playing for a period of months, or even years, and then suddenly stops working. Or that you enjoy reading both the Bible *and* the Koran. But be aware that the personal habits of your mentors and heroes are generally not applicable to your own development and happiness; there is no universal magic bullet. Most people are simply looking for answers to ancient questions, like: What are we doing here? What happens when we're not here? Are we really here? Half the fun is in seeking and stumbling upon the Truth, the Light, the Magic, the Better Bebop Solo; there are plenty of paths that lead there, and I can't tell you which to take. At least explore your options before you join a cult.

You may have to look no further than your chosen field for spiritual enlightenment. At its best, playing music in a group is a glorious celebration of the collective – of sacrifice for the greater good. *It don't mean a thing if you ain't cooperating!* Even when you practice or perform alone, you must harness your ego to your instrument and surrender yourself to the music you're playing. And music can heal, inspire, rile, and convert. (Just ask the music-hating Taliban.) Finally, music plays a vital role in almost all religions, and musicians are considered to be "close to God" in many cultures.

All I know is that for me, balance is the key:

I feel better when I exercise, eat well and get plenty of sleep.

I feel great when I help someone in need.

Hard work and fun complement one another.

I *need* to play and write music, read, work, travel and commune with nature.

My family and friends give meaning to it all. And they keep me in line.

To give and to receive love are good reasons to be alive.

I also believe in the Oakland Raiders. And the Tooth Fairy.

My grandmother gave me helpful advice: "If it hurts, think about something else."

I didn't have to pay a swami to teach me any of this.

Wedding Bells

No. Not someone else's. Yours, baby.

When I finally took the plunge, life got better. My marriage has a positive effect on my health, my music, my career, and my sense of well-being. And to seal the deal, my kids make sure that I don't get a chance to stare at my own navel for too long. Note that most dictionaries include a definition of the word "marriage" like "a close union," so I suppose you don't *have* to have a license. But it might help. Following are various reasons to get hitched and maybe even have a kid or two. To the relationship veterans and bitter divorcés and divorcées among you, please forgive the more basic reminders of the benefits of steady commitment:

1) You will have twice as much time for your music simply because you won't be out hunting for a mate. Don Wilkerson, an oft-inebriated elder statesman of the tenor saxophone, had an eloquently funky, unrepentantly sexist way of phrasing this: "What you put into the ladies at night, you take out of your horn during the day."

2) A good marriage raises both your self esteem and your serotonin levels.

3) It's worth the price of admission just to share your life with someone who has your best interests in mind, and to be able to bounce ideas off of someone you trust completely, day or night.

4) Since couples share the mundane duties and concerns of their daily lives, they have more time left over for the finer things. They usually have two heads and four hands. Sharing enhances your successes and softens your failures.

5) You live longer and healthier. This is confirmed by numerous long-term studies. It's worth a try.

6) My musician pals who have also been visited by the stork confirm that in addition to providing a new reason to live, their new babies also brought good financial karma. Could be the parents kicking in. Or perhaps when a freelancer has a new mouth to feed, his employers think, "Man … his poor baby's gonna starve. I should do the right thing and hire this guy." Or much more likely, the married father or mother becomes a more responsible person. Either way, being a dad is by far the coolest thing on my résumé.

But how do you find the love of your life? I think that you have to *be* the person you want to be before you'll find a mate who you want to be with. There are enough fish in the sea that you can wait for someone who radiates good vibes; who is happy, healthy, smart and loving; who has a good sense of humor, and knows how to compromise. It helps if they're autonomous, but not "missing in action" and don't feel compelled to compete with you. Find someone who is a team player, who shares your ability to give unselfishly. Just as musicians have to know when to be supportive and when to step into the spotlight, a good spouse knows when to be the moon and when to be the sun (or Mars or Venus). It helps if your partner loves music, doesn't mind your erratic schedule and "flexible" income, and functions well when you go on the road. Not that I was looking for perfection or anything …

If your partner is also a musician or if he or she does any kind of freelance work, be prepared for some difficult challenges, but enjoy the unspoken communication – the sympathetic vibes. Just don't start a band together – usually a recipe for disaster. Whatever happens, enjoy the quest, and … I almost forgot: I've got this great band for your wedding!

Escape From New York

Most musicians spend part of their careers on the road. This work provides a welcome change from the local gig grind, as well as steady (if temporary) income, and an opportunity to see a bit of the world. The penultimate tours pay megabucks, whisk you off to exotic locales in stylish private planes, have efficient tour management and abundant roadies, and put you up in fancy hotel suites. Unfortunately, most road gigs don't include such lavish perks.

When I was nineteen, I explored the highways and byways of the U.S. with Brother Jack McDuff in a small, sometimes rickety white truck in need of a paint job, helped lift his B-3 and leslie out of said blundermobile, and after a five-hour gig, pocketed $60 – when we played. It was tough, but playing jazz with McDuff was a beautiful thing: he was a living encyclopedia of swing; he taught me to play as though my life depended on it (as it often did); we played great music; we ate at superb soul food restaurants that I never could have found on my own; I saw the country in a way that can only be accomplished by extensive, truck-bound travel.

Indeed, as Jack Kerouac pointed out, the road can be addicting; you bust out of your rut, see new places, meet new people, and – if you're working – get paid for it. Some musicians are terminal party animals and the road is their ultimate sanctuary. Others enjoy playing music for new, diverse audiences. A high profile tour can also improve your work prospects back home. If you're lucky enough to be touring with your own band performing your own music, this is its own reward.

There are also plenty of drawbacks: despite being around and performing for big crowds, a poignant loneliness – longing to be home – is omnipresent; when you leave loved ones at home, long absences can undermine your relationships. It's hard to maintain disciplined practice and fitness routines. Playing the same music night after night can get boring. There are long hours spent at airports, in buses, at sound checks, in hotel lobbies; hurry-up-and-wait is the rule. Minor personality differences are amplified tenfold. And, of course, you won't be doing much sightseeing if your tour is cursed with a demanding road manager, itinerary, or rehearsal schedule. This is especially torturous in pretty cities, island paradises, and mountain retreats.

The typical road warrior must also struggle to find privacy, and time for quiet reflection. Your fellow road rats often take up a great deal of physical, aural, and karmic space, and urge you to "party" or simply annoy you with their collective hyperactivity. Don't join the fray, at least not all the time. Take up as little room as possible, and work diligently to maintain your discipline (practice, compose, read, exercise, explore your surroundings) and your equilibrium. Learn to shut out the din.

I find it helpful to use three criteria to determine the desirability of any job: 1) the quality of the music; 2) the people (I hope for warm, funny, energetic yet relaxed, smart colleagues who love life); and 3) the pay. I'll do a short job if any one of these elements is attractive, but I always hope for perfection in all three. Certainly if you're not making a lot of money, your level of satisfaction will largely depend on how much you enjoy the music and the musicians. I've had gigs that were so good that I forgot I was getting paid at all, and others where no amount of money could have compensated for the horrendous cacophony that surrounded me. Situations arise where you don't have to work hard, but fat paychecks are floating around and you want your share. Just be advised that anything that bugs you during early rehearsals and band meetings often becomes all-consuming once you're out on the road.

I'm not attempting to either advocate or condemn road work. Your tolerance for touring will be determined partly by the quality of the tour, and partly by your home life, age, and current career options. When you do go out, you will discover your own travel rhythms and develop methods for coping with the hardships.

Finally, even if you're a bona fide road rat, *you should take a vacation*. It's easy to be lulled into thinking that a week in Miami playing an American Express industrial show *is* a vacation. It is not. You must check out in earnest: leave your instruments and your iPhone behind. Go to a quiet place. You will recharge your batteries and gain badly needed perspective, which more than compensates for the expense of the trip and any lost work. If you don't have the cash for such an essential luxury, beg, borrow, and barter; *everyone* knows *someone* who knows *someone* with a little shack in the woods, or a ride you can hitch, or a dog you can dog-sit in return for the use of their apartment. The people I know who never take real vacations are certified wrecks.

If you live in a throbbing metropolis like New York or LA, you need to abandon ship more often. Though all the loud noise, type triple-A people, and the crowded, polluted conditions may effectively inspire you to create glorious music, it's just not enough.

TOP TEN SIGNS THAT IT'S TIME TO TAKE A BREAK:

10) You stay awake thinking of ways to maim and torture hecklers.

9) You drink more than you practice.

8) Your colleagues look at you with pity and say, "You need a vacation dude."

7) You don't remember how to play "Memories."

6) You finish playing "Freebird" and announce to the audience, "And now, ladies and gentlemen, we'd like to play a little ditty called "Freebird."

5) Groupies used to throw panties onto the stage, and now they throw beer bottles.

4) Your guitar glares at you and says, "Don't you *dare* touch me."

3) You leave your instrument at a club and don't realize it's missing until three days later.

2) During a performance of *Cats* you suddenly throw down your horn, jump out of the pit and start howling like a beagle.

1) Your cat asks you: "What did you say your name was?"

You and the Night and the Music

Remember to get a little sunshine – more than you get from gazing at the sunrise from the back of a cab after a night on the town. Of course, it's difficult to wake up at the crack of dawn when you just played a gig that began at midnight. And yes, I told you to go out and jam all night, to check out all the great musicians in the clubs, and to stay home and practice until your hands bleed. But none of it means much if you never see the light of day, and here's why: extensive data from long-term sleep research has proved that people who sleep during the night are healthier and live longer than those who sleep during the day. Combine a daytime sleeping habit with a little cigarette smoke, alcohol, and junk food, and you won't need heroin to kill you.

Are you dreaming of a good night's sleep? Though it's difficult to avoid vampire-like tendencies in our business, at least give yourself a fighting chance. If you know you have a few nights off, try to go to sleep earlier than usual. If you have a tough time getting to sleep, try to exercise more, avoid coffee and alcohol in the evening, and don't eat anything too close to bedtime. Read instead of watching TV. Try burning a candle with a relaxing scent like lavender. If little noises bother you – a common problem for musicians – wear earplugs when you hit the hay. Some people use "mindfulness" meditation before turning in. This type of meditation involves cultivating an acute awareness of present experience: you try to observe and concentrate on every detail of what you're doing at the moment, without making any "judgments." Finally, proceed with caution if you try sleep medicine, even if it's "natural."

The nightlife is enticing, and vampires are occasionally in vogue, but remember that even in a big city, two-thirds of the population is up-and-at-'em near the crack of dawn, and you'll never meet them (let alone get to work with them) if you sleep all day; many recording sessions start before noon; most "normal" businesses close at 5 p.m.; and living in the dark can lead to terminal SAD (Seasonal Affective Disorder). If you have a late-night gig and end up sleeping until 1 p.m., try to get outdoors for a walk before it gets dark.

Embrace the day!

The "Good" Old Days

It wasn't "all that." Really. The seductive memories of past gig glories and career triumphs can impair forward motion; the past often seems a little more glamorous than the present, but you should never attempt to repeat it.

First of all, sound is an elusive animal. We've all had those moments where we *thought* the band sounded great, only to later hear the truth revealed on playback. The magic of the moment is often based on emotion, not necessarily good musicianship. As time goes by, your tastes and priorities change; your hearing deteriorates or you become sensitive to loud sounds; your musical abilities usually improve; and you (hopefully) develop higher standards. If you could go back and listen to yourself play when you thought you were at your best – and when life was one big party – you might not be very impressed with what you heard. And if you're living in the past, you're not fulfilling your potential as a musician. Exploit and expand your current abilities; practice, play, and listen in the moment.

Of course, some things *were* better. There were nights when you had a great time *and* sounded phenomenal. You might justifiably miss a colleague or two. Maybe you used to play longer without getting tired, or you were able to hit higher notes on the trumpet. But at other times, the nirvana you remember is based on social interaction and not music. Your current feelings of inadequacy and nostalgia for the past usually have more to do with your physical condition than with your mental capacity. In fact, you know more about music now, and you also know how to forget what you know and just play. You're better at pacing yourself, reading audiences, and doing business. You have rich life experiences to draw from. You have more to say.

Many top musicians report that they rarely – if ever – listen to their old records or recordings of their live performances. This is partly because they're constantly growing and have reached new plateaus by the time their most recent recording is released. Some scholars argue that musicians and composers were better off prior to the advent of recorded music because they had to rely on their aural memories, which stimulated a more "pure" creativity; they probed the abstract and reached their own musical conclusions. Others go a step further and suggest that there was a progressive creative meltdown in the 20th century because musicians and composers recycled a glut of recorded ideas: single musical moments available on demand through the generations, endlessly imitated or watered down, resulting in a loss of urgency – of fire.

I don't embrace this philosophy. I love my record collection, and I wouldn't suggest that you toss yours. It's easy to listen to sounds from the past and still keep your ears (and your imagination) fresh: just listen to a wide variety of music so you don't get "stuck"; listen to musicians who were ahead of their time; don't listen to yourself (unless you're a beginner, or are making a record, or are judging the merits of your band's new song or last performance); and clear out your musical mind with regular periods (even weeks) of silence.

Don't leave the door open for nostalgia to creep in, at least where your music, your career, and perhaps your love life are concerned. As the great maestro of philosophy Kierkegaard pointed out, "Life can only be understood backwards; but it must be lived forwards." Repeat various mantras: "now's the time;" "just do it;" and "life is short." When you wake up in the morning (or late afternoon), think first of all the music you haven't made or heard yet, and get going. Play like you've never played before.

Remember Me?

This business of music is tough. Really tough. But then again, no one told you it would be easy. The fleeting panaceas of money and fame, and the soothing self-therapy of nostalgia are not enough to protect you from the inevitable slow periods you will encounter. Throughout this book I've attempted to point out many ways to find work, to capitalize on your achievements, and to stay busy. But the fact is, if you've achieved a certain level of success, repeating that success becomes increasingly difficult; the bigger you are, the harder you fall. Whether because of attrition or lost ambition, the glamour of a career in music can fade quickly.

There are many ways to become unemployed, regardless of the sparkle of your résumé: new people become powerful and hire their friends – you're not one of them; employers or audiences get bored and want to hire or hear something new; you offend someone and are unaware of it; someone is jealous of your success and spreads lies about you; your looks change; your instrument falls out of favor; people assume you're too expensive and don't bother to call in the first place; your family life takes over; the economy derails and entertainment dollars disappear. Depressed yet?

It's easy to blame your career nadirs on everything and everyone but yourself: you feel as if everyone should *know* how great you are by now, and miss you terribly; you imagine that people are spending their time thinking of ways to do you in; you criticize the music business, or make generalizations like "everyone's slow." Relax. Most people are too busy with their own lives to be thinking of you at all, let alone how to help or harm you. They're not suffering with you either. Some are busy with their families; others are working a lot. Also, if you make a promo call to an employer who is also experiencing a slow period, you run the risk of reminding him of his plight. Pick your promo targets carefully.

At times you'll feel as though you must do *something*. You decide that you're responsible for your own happiness, and that you must take control over your own destiny. Despite the fact that you're bummed – and sound like it – you call up one of your favorite employers, Ralph, who's thrown you a ton of work over the years.

"Hey Ralph. It's Fred. What's up?

"Hey Fred. What can I do for you?"

"Well, it's been a long time since we've worked together. Did I play a wrong note or something?"

"(laughs) Never, baby! Just haven't needed real strings lately."

"Hmmm. Hope that changes," you politely but urgently plead.

"Hey – me too. But listen, Fred, I gotta finish this track. I'll definitely keep you in mind. Let me know when you're performing, OK?"

"Cool."

"Great to hear from you, buddy." *Click.*

You give up. This is when you begin wondering why you didn't get yourself a law degree. Stop! Look! Listen!

Sure, you must *make* things happen, but you also should learn to *let* things happen. A period of unemployment is the perfect time to take a short break, reassess, and move forward. Treat it as a gift – you need downtime to gain perspective, and come up with a new plan of attack. Rank and file actors, dancers and basketball players have every right to complain – they face limited job opportunities during short careers in ridiculously crowded fields. Musicians are lucky because they can choose from a vast array of career paths, regardless of their current level of success or their age. You can reinvent your career on a dime: teach, start a transcription service, play on a cruise ship – do *something* music-related (see *Mommy, Where Do Gigs Come From?*). Devote more time to learning songs and transcribing solos. Or, just do something you enjoy for awhile; maybe you need a vacation. Try getting a "day job" to break the monotony, and to remind yourself of how privileged you are to be a musician. Sometimes all you need to do is lay low until the plague passes; many industry trends are cyclical. The one thing you can always count on is change. Learn to go with the flow. (See *One Good Discipline Deserves Another*, *Jammin' 'Til the Break of Dawn*, *Promote or Perish, Out of Sight ...*, and *Escape From New York* for other specific ideas of what to do when the chips are down.)

Don't quit unless you've exhausted all of your options. There are too many forces at play to rely on anything but your own savoir-faire; the "big call" may come 24 hours after your most miserable weekend, or it might take much longer, and thoroughly test your patience. Either way, you've got to be in it to win it. Make it a point to be the last one standing.

Abandon Ship!

The hours you spent working with the *Belwin Band Builder* paid off – big time. You've succeeded on many levels: you sound great; you play music you love with musicians who inspire you; you have money in the bank and money to burn; you have great friends and maybe even a beautiful house with a beautiful family and a prize-winning hamster in it. Are you happy? Or do you still feel empty – like you missed out on something? Maybe you're just tired of mixing music and commerce.

Your counterpart has been practicing for ten hours each day for 15 years and *still* can't make a living playing music.

Both of you might need the same medicine.

In previous sections I discussed the merits of developing new skills to compliment your music, moonlighting on other jobs to remind you of how lucky you are, and taking breaks and vacations. I've also touched upon the importance of finding inner peace and joy, which should always be the first item on the shopping list of life. But playing music *for a living* can take its toll. The music business can chew you up like a Labrador chews his slimy toy.

It might be time to try something else.

Consider trying another field – something that you've always dreamed of doing. Go back to school. Start a home business. Of course if you don't have financial resources you'll probably need to maintain a "normal" job while you gear up for your new endeavor, and the transition may take awhile. And finding any job during a recession can be tough. But most of the people I've talked with who have "checked out" of the music biz are somewhere between pleased and ecstatic with their decision. Over the years I've heard: "It's so refreshing to not have to deal with the bull anymore," and "My new business is so straight ahead: everyone knows their role and gets paid for it – on time," and "Now when I play music, I do it because I *want to*." You may find that pursuing a new career for a few years will renew your musical "innocence" – the love of music that made you skip parties to practice your instrument when you were a teenager.

It doesn't hurt to try. You can always rejoin the wacky world of entertainment later on. Or, if you're very lucky, turn your new gig into early retirement. But before you do anything rash, read the next section.

Why Are You (or Why Do You Want to Be) a Musician?

"We are a spectacular, splendid manifestation of life. We have language ... We have affection. We have genes for usefulness, and usefulness is about as close to a 'common goal' of nature as I can guess at. And finally, and perhaps best of all, we have music."

– Lewis Thomas in *The Medusa and the Snail* (1979)

Cash payments, free booze, and abundant companionship are enticing perks in the music world. It's a joyful revelation to a twelve-year-old boy that when he plays guitar, the finer specimens of the opposite sex pay more attention to him; the ability to seduce people with sound has caused many a young musician to practice diligently. Even Duke Ellington admitted that when he was young, he began playing ragtime piano because girls liked it. Most musicians also don't mind being the center of attention and receiving applause for it. And the relentless media blitz of images of rich entertainers has sparked more than a few careers in music. Perhaps when molecular biologists isolate the illusive music gene we'll have a tidy explanation for exactly what makes a musician.

Surely there are more noble inducements to pursue this life. What about our heroes? Well, while Johann Sebastian Bach and John Coltrane pursued higher calls, Franz Lizt and Charlie Parker definitely did not. Jimmy Hendrix perfected the art of early self-destruction, and some argue that he wouldn't have been as brilliant sans heroin. But I believe that all great artists experience epiphanies – sometimes multiple epiphanies – and moments of acute clarity that occur in spite of, and not because of their bad habits. Is it God calling? Maybe. In my best moments as a musician – when I'm in the "zone" – I feel like I'm not really there. I'm definitely not aware of my fingers on the instrument. (It's particularly sweet when this happens on a recording session because you get to hear evidence of your supernatural experience.) You know – flow; at-one with everything and everybody. And

I can assure you that despite my California roots, I'm not achieving this "magic" with mushrooms.

Beyond the creative rush are some practical perks: as a freelance musician you work with different people all the time, making for an exciting, unpredictable lifestyle; there's so much you need to work on during your "downtime" that you'll never become bored; you can be truly proud of yourself when things go well because you are your own boss; everything you do will contribute to the success of your one-man company; when you make mistakes or completely fail, you can adjust quickly since you know who and what the problems are; also, you will be unlikely to reprimand yourself as severely as a boss would in the 9-5 world.

Another good reason to be a musician is that you *are* a musician – that since you were young you've wanted to make music. If you have an unquenchable desire to play an instrument, do it. All the time. Chances are that you'll get good at it, especially if you have innate talent.

Until I was seven years old I was certain that I wanted to be an artist. Then a poet. But music was everywhere in my house: everyone in my family played at least one instrument; jam sessions were common; records and radios were playing all the time; music lessons were offered; practicing was encouraged – at times required. I used to linger long after school concerts and plays were over because I loved the lights, the sounds, and even the smell of the auditorium. My parents (though they were also fans of art and poetry) nourished my interest in music, and by the time I was thirteen, I knew I wanted to play professionally. I never again considered another job. This singular vision – this obsession – has guided me throughout my life, and helped me to ignore the inevitable ups and downs of a career in music.

If you're blessed with musical talent, disciplined enough to make good use of it, and lucky enough to turn it into a living, cherish the privilege. Even if musicians didn't have the power to heal, move, and inspire people, they would have a satisfying, potentially lucrative job with rigorous intellectual, creative, spiritual and physical challenges. And it can be done anywhere in the world. It's a great gig!

Thomas Carlyle put it eloquently:

"Music is well said to be the speech of angels; in fact, nothing among the utterances allowed to man is felt to be so divine. It brings us near to the infinite."

I think people feel this way when they truly love music. And true love is the best reason to do anything.

PART 5:
TALES FROM THE TRENCHES

Here are a few of my early career blunders and triumphs to entertain and hopefully enlighten you.

Baptism of Fire

Just after turning 18, I landed a tour with Ray Charles. I thought I had died and gone to heaven: fresh from the high school big band circuit, I was suddenly playing gorgeous arrangements with a band that included legendary musicians like trumpeter Johnny Coles; I traveled to exotic locales such as Woolongong, Australia to play for wildly enthusiastic audiences; I (innocently) dated a Raylette (one of Ray's backup singers) who all the guys were keen on; it was 1979 and I was making $575 per week on my first real job. I thought I'd reached the top.

As my confidence grew I convinced myself that I should be making more money – $650 per week, to be precise. I made an appointment to meet with the Genius.

In a hotel room in Phoenix, alone with one of the greatest artists of the 20th (and 21st) centuries, I learned two crucial career lessons. Thoroughly. Picture a green, newly anointed kid face-to-face with the Dragon Master – sightless but all-knowing – whose razor sharp mind and world famous head are in constant motion. As he rocked back and forth he spoke through Cheshire cat teeth:

"Now then. What can I do you for, Patch?" Everyone called me "Patch."

I mustered my courage and cautiously began, "Mr. Charles, I think …"

Already I'd committed two major faux pas: first, Ray wanted everyone to address him as Brother Ray, especially during business talks; second, the words *I think* ignited an animated 30 minute lecture where I learned that what *Brother Ray thinks* is all that matters, and that not only would I not be getting a raise, but that my job was in jeopardy.

Knees shaking and mouth dry, I left the room. One of the elder angels, organist James Polk, was waiting outside.

"How'd it go Patch?" asked the huge, lovely bear.

"Not so good," I replied.

"Now why do you s'pose that is?" queried Polk. I shook my head. He smiled and said, "Well, it ain't the money." Long pause. "No guesses? Alright. You didn't hear it from me, but just understand – it ain't the money." And then he walked away.

Two days later, my paramour ended our liaison, explaining that she too had been given a not so subtle warning. We stopped meeting; magically, my next paycheck was for $650.

MORAL: Never mix business with pleasure.

The Big Easy

After touring with Ray, I did a brief – very brief – stint at the Eastman School of Music. Rochester in the winter didn't match the glamour of the road, but I made good use of the semester by sitting in on graduate classes, listening and reading in the magnificent music library, composing for small ensembles, and perfecting my pool game. My only regret is that I didn't utilize the recording and keyboard facilities at Eastman's state-of-the-art studio; I could have gotten a jump on learning the technology that has transformed our industry. Anyway, New York City was so close I could taste it.

One day I got a message in my box at school from one of my schoolmates advising me that a group called L'il Queenie and the Percolators – in town from New Orleans – needed a sax player. I called the bandleader and agreed to do one show. We hit the stage that night, and from the first four cookin' bars of take-no-prisoners funk, I knew I had a home. L'il Queenie herself was Leigh Harris, a 4-foot 9 redheaded spitfire with great pipes – a superstar in the making. Members of the rhythm section would later start another legendary group, The Subdudes. Little Queenie and the Percolators *rocked*!

They liked me too, and asked if I could make a few more gigs in the area, and said that they might have an opportunity to headline at a hot new club in NYC. As the lure of academia quickly faded, I jumped at the chance. After a glorious week of playing at Rochester's clubs and crazy parties – during freshman finals – we boogied down to Manhattan.

"The 80's," a brand new club on the Upper East Side, was packed to the rafters in anticipation of L'il Queenie's arrival. The music press was out in force too. After a wild, cocaine frenzied night [the owner was later indicted on drug and record piracy charges] – and a rave review in the *Village Voice* that mentioned me in the first sentence – the band asked if I'd be willing to join them in New Orleans in a week or two. Despite having just arrived in the Big Apple, and having just met these dudes, I hightailed it back to Rochester to wrap up my school business and sent all my belongings to an address in Louisiana.

The keyboard player, John Magnie, called and told me to go back down to NYC and wait for him to mail me a plane ticket. With very little money in my pocket and only one change of clothes, I kicked around the city, living off the generosity of friends I'd made at Eastman and on the road. Two weeks went by. No ticket. During the third week I started street playing so I could eat – one of my top priorities.

Then the fateful call came: apparently the band already had a fine saxophonist who – being older and adverse to cold weather – "quit" right before the trip to Rochester. After the band returned to New Orleans they hired him back. John said he'd send my stuff back to New York, and that he was "sorry things didn't work out." Ouch.

There I was, alone in the big city – no college degree, no gig, no apartment and no clothes – all because I bought into that big pie in the sky. And I was profoundly disappointed not to be a Percolator. To add insult to injury, my boxes arrived from New Orleans *three months* later. But it all worked out: I was young, and I was in New York City.

MORALS: Look before you leap, especially when you're seduced by great music. If you don't get it in writing – or get a healthy advance, or at least know your employer well – make sure you have a solid contingency plan.

There is *No* Grass on the
Other Side of the Fence

In 1983 I joined a band called Slickaphonics: Ray Andersen, Mark Helias, Alan Jaffe, and Jim Payne. Our distinct brand of avant garde funk-jazz was popular in Europe, and we played every gig from the Montreux Jazz Festival to rock clubs in Hamburg and Berlin. Again, I was the kid. In addition to being older, stellar musicians, my cohorts were smart, creative, and funny. They had strong personalities and argued about every nuance of every note, not to mention every business decision – part of the joy of being a Slickaphonic. Most of all, they gave me an outlet to stretch, and encouraged me to push the envelope. Unfortunately, I didn't fully appreciate how lucky I was to be with this band.

After two tours and an album, the Slicks returned to New York to write and rehearse. During this period, an upstart pop-rock band, the Nude Ants, asked me to do a few club gigs, and to play on their new album. I wrote with the lead singer and their manager raised the cash to do a video of one of our songs. As MTV became more influential, dozens of fledgling pop groups like this one achieved real and overnight success. Delusions of grandeur filled my head – again.

Meanwhile, the Slicks were gearing up to go back to Europe, and I had to make a choice: stimulating art versus *potential* fame and fortune. Being young and stupid, I screwed up. The Nude Ants – woefully short on original ideas and functional management – imploded in short order. In retrospect, my decision was analogous to that of the white collar workers who abandoned their secure jobs in the late 1990s to join dot-com startups, only to see them crash and burn by the end of 2000.

Though the Slickaphonics argued themselves into oblivion within a year, I wish I'd been part of *their* debate.

MORAL: Musically fulfilling jobs are few and far in between. Hold on to them for dear life.

Nice Day For A White Wedding

In ancient times, before e-mails provided written evidence of gig details, I got a call from a clubdate office to play solo saxophone for a wedding ceremony at a church on lower Fifth Avenue in New York. The job entailed waiting outside the church; when the doors opened at 11am, I was to play a jazzy version of Mendelssohn's "Wedding March," the classic wedding recessional. The newlyweds would hustle down the steps in a hail of rice, laughter, and joyful saxophonistics – an easy gig by any measure.

This particular Sunday morning was damp and gray, and there was a chance of a shower. I showed up early to get the lay of the land, and find out where I should play if it started raining. With the exception of a few pedestrians, no one was around, and I thought it was best not to enter the church in case the ceremony was in progress.

At 10:57, I focused all my attention on the church doors, horn at the ready. At the stroke of 11, a fellow in a dark suit slowly opened the doors; he didn't see me, and he hustled back inside before I could flag him down to get an update. Something felt wrong. A moment later, I saw several people coming towards the exit, so I busted into my swingin' take on the happy tune. Heads turned, and I thought I heard a woman scream. Just as I really start jamming, I heard someone yell: "Stop that right now! Get out of here! What in the hell are you doing?" Another guy comes running down the steps, looking like he was going to try to tackle me. I hustled my vintage Selmer to safety, and braced for a confrontation. The angry fellow bellowed:

"I don't know who you are or why you would play such a sick joke, but you should leave right now or you're going to get hurt."

Assessing my options, I made a gentle inquiry: "Isn't this the Parker wedding?"

"Listen to me carefully, young man. I don't know where you're supposed to be, or who sent you here, but you've just ruined this *funeral*. Leave now."

I could see the casket coming down the stairs behind him.

"I'm so sorry," I offered. "Apparently they sent me to the wrong church."

"Leave!"

I quickly packed up, and escaped down the block to a pay phone. I called the clubdate office and left the gory details on the machine, then beeped-in to get my messages. After several vitriolic diatribes from the boss ("Where the fuck are you? You're fuckin' late!"), there was a long apology from Jenny, the office manager, followed by a short apology from the boss. It began to rain; I was wearing a nice suit, so I treated myself to lunch at a swank restaurant and called it a day.

MORALS: Confirm and reconfirm the job details. E-mail and cell-phones are a musician's best friends.

Game Over

Avoid traction. The quickest way to impair or end your career is by playing too hard. I love sports. But my third broken bone was a doozy. It always happens the same way: an evil little voice tells you to make that last run down the slope; it's icy now that the sun has gone down; you're tired and reckless; you go too fast and end up in an asymmetrical heap at the bottom of the hill. My swan song as a jock was a high-speed sled accident that split my humerus in two. Not humorous! It took eight months to heal, followed by four months of physical therapy. My arm, hand, back, neck, and shoulder have never been quite the same. Sledding was never *that* much fun. Cross-country skiing is better exercise anyway.

Repetitive stress injuries are even more common than sled accidents. In addition to the bizarre body positions required to play most instruments, musicians carry heavy loads to and from their work-places. You can do a lot to help prevent injuries caused by your nor-mal routine: stretch or do yoga exercises before and after you play your instrument; use good posture at all times, and avoid putting pressure on your lower back; invest in a good chair to sit in when you practice or do other work; get up and walk around frequently; take Alexander Technique classes; drink lots of water and get enough cal-cium. Prevention is the key to good health.

While you're at it, take the necessary steps to protect your hearing: permanent hearing loss is a common occurrence in our profession. Since hearing loss is usually gradual and painless, you may become disabled before you know something is wrong. Consult your doctor, and talk to colleagues who use custom ear plugs. Stay as far away as possible from cymbals, speakers, and other ear shattering devices. Keep your headphone volume low. Find a time and place for com-plete silence to give your ears a well-deserved rest.

MORALS: You're not Michael Jordan. Plan for the long haul. Protect your extremities and your hearing.

Spilled Champagne

Every so often you will be presented with a fabulous artistic or business opportunity. Learn to recognize these gifts and to seize the moment: you make your own breaks.

Without going into gory detail, let's just say that I've squandered more than my share of potential glory, and that I feel lucky to have been given second, third, and even fourth chances. My mistakes have ranged from the silly to the disastrous: being in a small room with a few dozen of the most important people in the business and not managing to muster the moxie to talk with any of them; not return-ing phone calls promptly; saying no to playing gigs that *sounded* like they would be a drag, but resulted in propelling the participants to stardom; not pursuing my colleagues' suggestions ("you should really call so and so"); failing to defray minor misunderstandings; failing to rebuild broken bridges.

There were also numerous occasions when I neglected to gather enough information about a gig I accepted, or when I played non-union recording sessions – known as "dark dates" or "buyouts." Unfortunately, they are increasingly common. But you sure feel like a chump when one of these sessions yields a hit record, film, or long running jingle with *no residuals* (a.k.a. royalties or "back end"). Talk about being your own worst enemy . . . Being "too friendly" or acquiescent never seems like a sin when you're doing it. But after some wolf in sheep's clothing calls you and asks if you'll play a "quick solo and a few horn parts on a track that will probably go nowhere" and laments that "I'm working with a nonexistent budget and I can't pay you what you're worth," and when you turn on your TV and hear your solo on that track for the 99th time, you will understand the value of the words "no thanks." There is stuff I played on twenty years ago that still haunts me via satellite. Qué será será, rats, phooey, and to hell with it all.

It's also a mistake to complain too much. There are many musicians and singers who would be thrilled to even be *considered* for a big job, who *enjoy* hearing themselves on the radio (even when it doesn't pay), and who don't enjoy listening to a successful musician moan about the glory he *didn't* have. Complaining is often worse than boasting.

To put it gently, I've created a large repertoire of faux pas from which to learn. Below is a list of rules I learned the hard way. I assume that you'll take care of the obvious: playing and looking your best, saying and doing the "right thing," and being reliable, amiable and helpful.

1) Exhibit grace under pressure. If you're in over your head – say you're backstage and don't feel so good and someone introduces you to a famous producer – pull yourself together. Take a deep breath and put on a happy face; you only have to be "with it" for a couple of minutes. Also, this fellow *knows* you want to work with him. Show some enthusiasm and respect, but don't gush and never beg.

2) Go to as many industry parties as you can tolerate.

3) When someone invites you to sit in with them, do it.

4) Make those calls. Now. You know, those tough calls to powerful, difficult people who can make or break you. You have nothing to lose.

5) Parlay "mid-level gigs" into "big gigs," and "big gigs" into "dream gigs"; there's no better time to find great jobs than when you're already working. Hand out your CD; call or e-mail producers, contractors, and managers inviting them to hear the band you're playing with; talk to equipment manufacturers about an endorsement; collaborate with the songwriters you meet at your gigs and write songs for the artists you're working with.

6) What's "important" can change: sometimes it's your art, other times it's your health or happiness. Once in a while you have to focus exclusively on business and commerce. Hopefully you'll learn to recognize those pivotal points before your potential employer's eyes glaze over during your over-detailed description of your music or of your recent trip to Paris. Keep it simple. And if you're going through a particularly negative phase, either learn to turn on the instant charm or stay away from influential people until you get a grip.

7) Stay in touch with the people who you've worked with. Thank the people that have helped you, and try to return favors even if it takes years to accomplish. Never assume that someone doesn't "need" the work, or doesn't appreciate your gratitude. Just making the effort means a lot.

8) Be aware that when you feel that the music business is doing you in, you may be having a subjective episode; things aren't always as bad as they seem. And when they are, you're in good company.

9) Pay attention! Golden opportunities don't always announce themselves with a fanfare.

10) There are some things that you can't control – or even influence. Know when to lay low, or when to give up.

11) Don't dwell on your failures. Instead, concentrate on creating opportunities and realizing your full potential.

MORALS: In business, your maturity and tenacity are at least as important as the quality of your work. Know that everything is not about *you*. And be prepared; strike while the iron is hot.

Bright Moments

After all that confessin' I thought I'd allow myself a little horn blowin'. Below are some of the bright moments that have made me feel lucky to be alive and even luckier to be a musician. I hope you've already experienced or will experience similar good fortune.

I played at the Monterey Jazz Festival for three years as part of the California High School All-Star Band, and in various small groups. Each year, composers and performers like Thad Jones, George Duke, Benny Golson and Dave Friesen would write new material, and fly in to rehearse and perform with us. It was a surreal experience to be 16, on stage in front of fifteen thousand people, and playing *real* music with *real* musicians. It was around this time that I decided that a career in music might be better than a job at Arnell's Pizza.

By the time I was 19, I'd played on a handful of records, but I'd never played on a hit. That year I did a record with Brother Jack McDuff called *Kisses* (Sugar Hill). I'll never forget how good it felt to hear the title track on the radio for the first time. Inside of four minutes and thirty-three seconds my complexion cleared up for good.

A few years later, I found myself on stage at the Montreux Jazz Festival with the Slickaphonics. As we performed our avant-garde funk for a SRO crowd, the great Keith Haring painted a giant mural behind us. [If you have a photo or a video of this performance, please get in touch.] During that same tour, a photo of me next to the King of Norway appeared on the front page of the biggest Norwegian newspaper, and the Slickaphonics made the cover of the French magazine *Jazz*. Being recognized on the streets of Oslo and

Paris in the same month was a trip. Now I *knew* I had picked the right job.

The good fairy struck again when I was on stage at Mikell's with Who It Is (Cornell Dupree, Richard Tee, Will Lee and Steve Gadd). It was Cornell and Irma Dupree's 25th wedding anniversary and both Stevie Ray Vaughan and George Benson were in the house; *both* of them had their guitars. Now if you ever had the pleasure of hearing any *one* of these guys play in an informal setting, you've heard some *happening* guitaristics. But put Dupree, Vaughan and Benson together ... it blew the roof off the building. That night I learned how to "trade fours" like never before. A few weeks later, we played at the old Lone Star on 5th avenue, and Tom Jones sat in to sing "It's Not Unusual" and about fifty other songs; the band sounded so good that he didn't want to stop. We didn't mind though: it was the first time our female fans had ever thrown their panties onstage.

1985 and 1986 were particularly good years for me. I played in the pit band for Bob Fosse's last show, "Big Deal," with legendary composer and arranger Ralph Burns aboard. Each night after the final curtain, I flew over to my gig with the Playboy Club house band. During the day, I played on records and jingles, and recorded original material courtesy of an award from the National Endowment for the Arts. To top it off, I went on tour with Steve Winwood. The *opening acts* were Bruce Hornsby, Level 42, and Jimmy Cliff. Backstage visitors included many of the top music and film stars of the day, but Elton John was the most noticeable: he arrived at a show in full regalia via helicopter.

I've done a lot of TV gigs, but playing in the house band for Joy Behar's "Way Off Broadway" was particularly cool. Joy was generous and funny, and our MD, the legendary Rick Derringer, took no prisoners. Our very easy job was to back up a wide range of artists à la the Letterman band, but with a virtuoso rock star in the driver's seat. He showcased everybody in the band, and no matter how hard he had partied the previous night, his song count-offs into and out of commercials were always perfect. Plus, he played the hell out of the guitar. "Rock & Roll Hoochie Koo" never sounded better.

One of my favorite gigs was very brief. Back in the day when the security procedures at Manhattan's popular landmarks were relatively simple, I was hired to bring my horn to the observation deck of the Empire State Building, and play "Someday My Prince Will Come" as my employer dropped to his knees and proposed to his girlfriend. It was a lovely summer evening; she was completely surprised, and after shedding tears of joy, cried "Yes, yes yes!"; the tourists and building personnel applauded enthusiastically. It was positively cinematic. A short, fun, well-paid gig in the service of romance, with a nice view to boot: what more could you ask for?

If I had to pick one recording session that I'm most proud of (so far), it would be the one I did for the film *Hairspray*. It wasn't so much the music *or* the bread that made it so sweet. It's that I got to play on a soundtrack for a cult film by *John Waters* – an institution. I felt like I was on top of the world when I went to the premier with my date, and heard my *big* solo during one of the film's *big* moments.

Throughout the years, I've had the privilege of performing at numerous schools, hospitals, nursing homes, mental institutions, and prisons. I've led wild jam sessions at preschools, played concerts for the inmates at Rikers Island, and held clinics and master classes at high schools and colleges throughout the world. I played a regular gig at the Cerebral Palsy Center in Manhattan, did dozens of gigs for Hospital Audiences, Inc., and play annually at Ronald McDonald House. This is by far the most meaningful, most fulfilling work that I do.

In 2005 I joined nineteen "heavy hitters" from New York, LA, and Nashville for a thoroughly enjoyable week of jams, rehearsals, concerts, and recordings at the Rhythmic Music Conservatory in Copenhagen. Each of us arranged a few rock, R&B, jazz, and pop songs, and led twenty separate bands consisting of talented and charming college students, all of whom attended the school at no cost. The week culminated in several excellent studio recordings with accompanying videos, a burning faculty concert, and a great night of music by the student bands.

Ultimately, though, I'd be lost without my current private students, and the hundreds of students I've taught over the years; they're my fountain of youth.

Finally, I've had the good fortune to have led and played in many bands comprised of extraordinary musicians, and to have performed for thousands of truly appreciative people. From playing for the devoted jazz fans in Tübingen, to playing for the screaming teens at

Madison Square Garden, I've lived a charmed life. Yes, it's a tough job, but *somebody's* gotta do it!

It's all enough to give you a big head. But if music doesn't humble you, the music business definitely will, so enjoy the feathers while they're still in your cap.

AFTERWORD

As you, your music and your career develop, I hope you will revisit different parts of this book. During your inevitable triumphs and tribulations – and when you find yourself lost in the vast gray areas between music for its own sake, music for fun, and music for money – it might be comforting to know that others have been there before you, and survived to tell the tale. But remember that whether you're a superstar or a beginner, no one can take away your love for music, the joy you experience when you play, or the good times you have with your fellow musicians.

"I just want to play. Let someone else worry all that other stuff."

Not a bad idea. I was definitely not thinking about "all that other stuff" on my most recent gig: when you make music, too much thinking of any kind can impede creativity, spontaneity, musical ESP, and clear self-expression; you must disappear and become the music. So it might be a good idea to find a manager and an agent to handle some of your business affairs so that you can *really* disappear. Furthermore, all the reading, thinking, and business expertise in the world won't make you *play* better. Either you've got "it" or you don't, right?

Not so fast: it's more like "sometimes you've got it and sometimes you don't." Maybe you're only as good as your last gig, but you can come roaring back on the next one; and the definition of "it" can change. Sometimes your real muse won't show up for years. Plus, what you do *in between* your gigs is critical, and that's what most of this book is about.

I have two more pieces of advice for you. First, cherish your innocence: don't let the rough and tumble business of music harden you to beauty. Find beauty anywhere you can – in the rhythm of the city, in the melodies of birds, in the sound of silence, in the music of the spheres. Second, beware your inner critic. That critic can be a good friend – the insightful one who tells you the truth, the one who makes you laugh at yourself and deflates your delusions.

But don't fall in love with this friend: he can also provide you with excuses to procrastinate, lose hope, and fail; don't allow yourself to enjoy self-criticism more than you enjoy your work. Know your friends and enemies: know yourself.

OK. Enough drama. Enough advice. Who in their right mind would not want to be able to play an instrument and write songs? No matter how you look at it, musicians have it made. If you've enjoyed your journey half as much as I've enjoyed mine, you'll know exactly what I'm talking about.

Made in the USA
Charleston, SC
22 March 2012